ACT® Elements

Middle School Math
Teacher Manual

MasteryPrep

ACT® is the registered trademark of ACT Inc. MasteryPrep has no affiliation with ACT Inc., and ACT® Elements is not approved or endorsed by ACT Inc.

© Copyright 2018 MasteryPrep.

All Rights Reserved. No part of this publication may be reproduced, stored in a retrieval system, distributed, or transmitted in any form or by any means, including photocopying, recording, or other electronic or mechanical methods, without the prior written permission of the publisher. For permission requests, write to the publisher, addressed "Attention: Permissions Coordinator," at the address below.

Inquiries concerning this publication should be mailed to:

MasteryPrep
7117 Florida Blvd.
Baton Rouge, LA 70806

MasteryPrep is a trade name and/or trademark of Ring Publications LLC.
This publication, its author, and its publisher are in no way affiliated with or authorized by ACT Inc. ACT® is a copyright and/or trademark of ACT Inc.

10　9　8　7　6　5　4　3　2　1

ISBN-13: 978-1-948846-34-9

Table of Contents

Introduction 5

Operations: Word Problems, Part 1 11

Operations: Word Problems, Part 2 13

Operations: Word Problems, Part 3 15

Percents, Part 1 17

Percents, Part 2 19

Percent Change 21

Proportions 23

Polygon Area 27

Ratios 29

Exponents 31

Graphs and Charts: Word Problems 33

Absolute Value 35

Inequalities 38

Sequences 41

Substitution 43

Linear Equations 46

Modeling Equations: Word Problems 49

Solving Equations: Word Problems 51

Average, Median, and Mode, Part 1 54

Average, Median, and Mode, Part 2 56

Counting 58

Probability, Part 1	60
Probability, Part 2	62
Data Interpretation	64
Factors, Part 1	66
Factors, Part 2	68
Fractions, Part 1	71
Fractions, Part 2	74
Perimeter and Line Segments, Part 1	77
Perimeter and Line Segments, Part 2	79
Circle Area and Circumference, Part 1	81
Circle Area and Circumference, Part 2	83
Deconstructing Geometric Figures	86
Measurement Relationships	89
Volume, Part 1	93
Volume, Part 2	95

Introduction

Elements Math

The Elements program is designed to provide middle school and high school teachers with daily questions that emphasize practice in each of the four subject areas on the ACT and Aspire tests. The goal of Elements is to provide everything necessary to administer effective and efficient bell ringers for classes in English, math, reading, and science.

Each question in the Elements program has been carefully modelled after the difficulty and style of ACT and Aspire questions, assuring a high fidelity to the test content. Each grade-level appropriate skill included in the program was chosen following a deep analysis of real ACT and Aspire tests.

ACT and Aspire Math Subtest Overview

ACT	Aspire 6	Aspire 7	Aspire 8
Number of questions: 60 questions	**Number of points:** 46 points on 34 questions	**Number of points:** 46 points on 34 questions	**Number of points:** 53 points on 38 questions
Amount of time given: 60 minutes	**Amount of time given:** 60 minutes	**Amount of time given:** 60 minutes	**Amount of time given:** 65 minutes
Score range: 1–36	**Score range:** 400–451	**Score range:** 400–453	**Score range:** 400–456

Since the questions on the Aspire may be worth multiple points, it is easier to talk to students about the number of *points* on the test as opposed to the number of *questions*. This does not affect their pacing strategy as outlined in the book, but it helps bring clarity to the scoring system so they can better understand their goal scores.

The math subtest is designed to measure a student's ability to understand a broad range of mathematical topics. There are five types of items on the math test.

Pre-Algebra: These are word problems that require students to perform basic mathematical tasks. Students might need to add, subtract, multiply, or divide, find a percent, or work out an average.

Elementary Algebra: These basic algebra problems can be solved by using the FOIL method, by factoring, or by setting up an equation with variables.

Plane Geometry: These problems ask students to solve problems involving area, perimeter, volume, angles, triangles, and other shapes.

Intermediate Algebra: These problems involve complex inequalities, complex numbers, systems of equations, and matrices.

Coordinate Geometry: These problems involve coordinate planes, slopes, y-intercepts, and coordinates.

Pacing: There is an inherent order of difficulty on the math test. As a result, students are best advised to move quickly—but accurately—through the first half of questions and to spend more time on the second half.

Students should attempt the sections in order, from beginning to end, working questions as they go. They should be prepared to make educated guesses on questions they find difficult, even early on in the test. Students should be especially prepared to have difficulty working the last few questions, though they should still find time to attempt them and leave nothing blank, no matter the circumstance.

Elements Anatomy

Exercises

The Elements Math workbook is designed to be implemented as daily bell ringers. Each exercise constitutes one bell ringer. The Elements Math workbook contains 180 exercises in total, meaning 180 days of bell ringer activities.

There are two types of exercises in Elements Math: question sets and free-response activities.

Question Sets make up the majority of the exercises. Each weekly set of exercises contains four question sets. Each question set contains two or three practice questions that are tightly modelled after the style and content of real ACT or Aspire questions. Some of these questions are multiple choice, while others are in the form of a constructed response.

Free-Response Activities always come as the last exercise of a weekly set. These exercises present ACT and Aspire content in a written, free-form activity that encourages students to use creative reasoning. The purpose of the activities is to broaden the students' understanding of the core concepts that are frequently assessed on the ACT and Aspire.

Weekly Sets

Each exercise belongs to a weekly set of five exercises. The weekly sets are broken down in the following manner:

	Exercise 1	2–3 Multiple-Choice Questions
	Exercise 2	2–3 Multiple-Choice Questions
Math	Exercise 3	2 Constructed Response Questions
	Exercise 4	2 Constructed Response Questions
	Exercise 5	Free-Response Activity

Pacing

Each exercise may be paced differently depending on the skill level of the class, but it should follow this general pace:

Class Instruction	30 seconds
Exercise Delivery	3 minutes
Exercise Review	2 minutes

Review

Once the class has completed an exercise, review the results. For practice questions, reveal the correct answers to each question. Then explain the process of selecting the correct answer as well as eliminating incorrect answers when appropriate. For activities, lead a brief discussion about the exercise before tying it back to the ACT or Aspire.

Elements Best Practices

Reviewing Versus Teaching: As Elements exercises are intended to be used as bell ringers, it is recommended that you do not use them as teaching curriculum. Instead, review the explanations of the questions briefly before moving into your daily lesson content. However, if you decide that your class could use more instruction, it makes sense to spend time remediating the content required to answer the questions. You will find the most success with the program if you determine whether to review or to teach prior to implementation of the exercises.

Write in the Book: Students should write in the book for each of the exercises. In this way, they can practice test-taking techniques that would be appropriate for the ACT or Aspire tests. It will also support informal evaluation of the class during the bell ringers and formal evaluation of individual students if desired.

Test Preparation Strategies: Since the ACT and Aspire tests are standardized, it is recommended that you use the Elements exercises to reinforce good test-taking techniques. While there are many strategies that MasteryPrep endorses, you should emphasize the following strategies in all exercises for all subjects:

Mark and Move – If students get stuck on one of the questions, they should practice marking in their books, selecting their best guesses, and then moving on to the next question.

Process of Elimination – Students should practice eliminating answers whenever possible, especially on English, reading, and science questions. Elimination techniques should also be used on math exercises when appropriate.

Pacing – Students should be encouraged to spend the appropriate time on each question according to the pacing guide. This will help them to understand the pacing of the ACT and Aspire tests.

Never Leave a Blank – Students should practice never leaving a question blank, even if they are unsure how to answer it. The ACT and Aspire do not penalize for guessing, so it is always in a student's interest to make an educated guess.

Test Preparation Inclusion: If, in addition to the Elements program, your school is using test preparation materials such as MasteryPrep's ACT Mastery Basic or Advanced programs, you should coordinate with the ACT or Aspire Prep instructors to make sure that your overall advice coincides with the advice given in those classes.

Operations: Word Problems, Part 1

Exercise 1 (pg. 6)

1. **The correct answer is D.** Add the three numbers together to get 821. Here, 2 is in the tens place. Round 821 down to 820.

2. **The correct answer is K.** Subtract the average temperature of Antarctica from the average temperature of Death Valley.

   $57 - (-89) = 57 + 89 = 146$

   The average temperature of Death Valley is 146°C greater than the average temperature of Antarctica.

3. **The correct answer is D.** Subtract the final temperature from the initial temperature.

   $5 - (-14) = 5 + 14 = 19$

   The temperature decreased by 19°F.

Exercise 2 (pg. 7)

1. **The correct answer is B.** First convert weeks to days. Afterwards, divide the total revenue gained by the number of days.

   5 weeks · 7 days per week = 35 days

   $70,000 ÷ 35 days = $2,000 per day

   The average daily funding raised is $2,000.

2. **The correct answer is G.** Since Winston gave $2 on the first day, subtract 2 from 46 to get 44. Winston gives $4 per day every day after the first, so divide by 4 to get the number of days after the first day.

   44 ÷ 4 = 11 days

   Winston will give $46 on the 11th day after the first day, so it will be the 12th day.

3. **The correct answer is D.** Divide the total cost of the plant soil by the total pounds of plant soil.

   $20 ÷ 8 pounds = $2.50 per pound

   So, the cost for a pound of plant soil is $2.50.

Exercise 3 (pg. 8)

1. The student added the numbers correctly to obtain 1,139. However, the student rounded to the hundreds place instead of the tens place. The student should know that the digit in the tens place is 3, so rounding in the tens place would result in 1,140.

2. The answer is incorrect because the student divided the amount of bags by the cost. Instead, the student should divide the cost by the number of bags. This would give the correct answer, $2.

Exercise 4 (pg. 9)

1. Find the number of days in 4 weeks:

   Multiply the number of weeks by 7 days per week, 4 · 7 = 28 days.
   Divide the number of sheets by the number of days.
   This gives 595,000 ÷ 28 = 21,250.

   On average, 21,250 sheets are printed daily.

2. Since the coldest temperature of Mercury is 1,080°F colder than the hottest temperature 800°F, the coldest temperature can be found by subtracting 1,080°F from 800°F.

   800°F − 1,080°F = −280°F

Exercise 5 (pg. 10)

1. Answers will vary.

Operations: Word Problems, Part 2

Exercise 1 (pg. 11)

1. **The correct answer is E.** Calculate the total number of slices eaten by the three friends and add 2 to determine the number of slices that make up half the pie. Then multiply the result by 2 to determine how many slices make up the whole pie.

   3 + 2 + 1 + 2 = half the slices in the original pie

   8 = half the slices in the original pie

   8 · 2 = 16 slices in original pie

2. **The correct answer is F.** The temperature decreases by 3°F for 4 hours, or a total of 3 · 4 = 12°F overall. Subtract 12°F from −5°F.

   −5 − 12 = −17°F

3. **The correct answer is B.** On day 1, the teacher gave the students 3 words, while on days 2 through 9, or 8 more days, the teacher gave the students 2 words per day.

   3 + 2(8) = 3 + 16 = 19 words total in the first 9 days

Exercise 2 (pg. 12)

1. **The correct answer is C.** For the first 35 hours, Elena is paid $14.00/hour. For the next 7 hours (42 − 35 = 7), she is paid (1.5)($14/hour), or $21/hour.

   (35)($14) + 7($21) =

   $490 + $147 = $637

2. **The correct answer is J.** Determine the total ounces of milk that Trevor bought, then find how many 12-ounce cartons of milk this would be equivalent to.

   8 ounces · 16 cartons · 6 boxes = 768 ounces of milk

   $\frac{768}{12}$ = 64 12-ounce cartons of milk

3. **The correct answer is A.** Find the total decrease in value and divide by the number of years, 5.

   $22,400 − $17,800 = $4,600

   $\frac{\$4,600}{5}$ = $920

Exercise 3 (pg. 13)

1. If the temperature increases by 3°F for 4 hours, it will increase by 12°F total from the original temperature, or 65°F + 12°F = 77°F.

2. The student did not incorporate the different rates she is paid into her calculation of her income that week. The correct answer is:

    ($10)(15) + ($15)(12)

    $150 + $180 = $330

Exercise 4 (pg. 14)

1. Calculate the amount of pieces in half of the cake by adding all of the pieces Fred, Nora, and Lily took plus the 4 extra pieces.

    4 + 2 + 3 + 4 = 13 pieces of cake

    Double this to get the total number of pieces in the cake.

    13 · 2 = 26 total pieces.

2. The house increased in value by $148,500 − $120,500 = $28,000 total over the course of 7 years.

    $\frac{\$28,000}{7}$ = $4,000 average increase per year.

Exercise 5 (pg. 15)

1. Map depictions will vary, but the direction to the chocolate shop is southeast from the start.

Math Elements: Middle School Bell Ringers Teacher Manual

Operations: Word Problems, Part 3

Exercise 1 (pg. 16)

1. **The correct answer is B.** First add the values given in the question.

   146 + 221 + 576 = 943

   Note that 943 is less than 950, and thus rounds down to 900.

2. **The correct answer is J.** For the temperature to cool from 23°F to 0°F, the temperature would fall 23°F. To cool from 0°F to −8°F, the temperature would fall 8°F. Thus to cool from 23°F to −8°F, the temperature would need to fall by 23°F + 8°F = 31°F.

3. **The correct answer is E.** In order to solve for the average speed in miles per hour, divide the total number of miles traveled by the total hours spent driving.

   288 ÷ 4 = 72 miles per hour.

Exercise 2 (pg. 17)

1. **The correct answer is D.** First find the total amount of cookies by multiplying the amount of boxes by the amount of cookies per box.

   5 · 12 = 60 cookies

   Next divide the total amount of cookies by the amount of people to find out how to evenly distribute the amount of cookies.

   60 ÷ 6 = 10 cookies per person

2. **The correct answer is K.** In order to find the total amount of money to spend on pizzas, multiply the price of an individual pizza by the amount of pizzas you will buy.

   4 · 14 = $56

3. **The correct answer is E.** The best way to solve this problem is to work backwards.

   If Travis has 76 cards and Tucker has half as many cards as Travis, then Tucker has 76 ÷ 2 = 38 cards.

   If Tucker has 38 cards amd Timothy has three times as many cards as Tucker, then Timothy has 38 · 3 = 114 cards.

Exercise 3 (pg. 18)

1. The first part of the questions suggests that on average each carpenter takes 5 hours to build one dresser. Thus given 100 carpenters building at the same rate of each carpenter producing 1 dresser in 5 hours, it would take 5 hours to build 100 dressers.

2. The distributive property is used by multiplying the outside value by each of the individual inside values.

   $4(9x) - 4(7) = 36x - 28$

Exercise 4 (pg. 19)

1. Set up an equation using the price of the ball as the variable x.

   $(x) + (x + 1) = \$1.10$

   $2x + 1 = \$1.10$

   $2x = \$0.10$

   $x = \$0.05$

   The ball costs $0.05, and since the bat costs 1 dollar more, the bat costs $1.05.

2. The house would be half covered in flies after 47 days.

   If the house is completely covered in 48 days and the flies double every day, then that means that one day previous to being completely covered the house was half covered.

Exercise 5 (pg. 20)

1. Possible answers include but are not limited to:

   $L = 4 + M$

   $M = 2J$

   $L = 4 + 2J$

   $R = M - 3$

   $R = 2J - 3$

   $L + M + J + R = m$

   $4 + 2M + J + R = m$

   $L + 2J + J + R = m$

   $L + 2M + J - 3 = m$

Percents, Part 1

Exercise 1 (pg. 21)

1. **The correct answer is D.** In order to solve for the missing value, multiply the total number of points by the percentage that Michelle wants to earn.

   50 · 0.90 = 45 points

2. **The correct answer is H.** Solve for the value of the tip by multiplying the total bill by the percent of the bill representing the value of the tip.

   125 · 0.2 = $25

3. **The correct answer is B.** Multiply the original value by the decimal representation of the percentage. Remember that percent values can be converted to the decimal representation by dividing by 100.

   2.75 · 60 = 165

Exercise 2 (pg. 22)

1. **The correct answer is A.** Multiply the original value by the decimal representation of the percentage. Percent values can be converted to decimal representations by dividing by 100.

   80 · 0.04 = 3.2

2. **The correct answer is G.** The chart shows the percentages for the different heights, so to find the percent taller than 66 inches, add the percentages higher than 66 inches.

   26% + 8% + 2% = 36%

3. **The correct answer is C.** 90 students out of a total of 200 students chose blue. So the fraction of students who chose blue is given by the following: $\frac{90}{200}$ simplifies to $\frac{45}{100}$, or 0.45, showing that 45% chose blue.

Exercise 3 (pg. 24)

1. The student actually solved for 40% of 80, as 0.4 · 100% = 40%. 4% = 0.04, so the student should multiply by this value instead.

   0.04 · 80 = 3.2

2. $25.00 + ($25.00)(0.2) = $30.00

   The first part of the total bill is the value of food bought, which is $25.00. The tip is 20% of the $25.00, or (0.2)($25.00) = $5. Adding the two values yields the total bill after applying a 20% tip, which is $30.00.

Exercise 4 (pg. 25)

1. $150 - 105 = 45$

    $\dfrac{45}{150} = 0.3$

    $0.3 \cdot 100\% = 30\%$

    First find the total number of students surveyed that prefer baked potatoes by subtracting the students that prefer mashed potatoes from the total. Next create a fraction using the number of students that prefer baked potatoes as the numerator and the total students surveyed as the denominator. This fraction, after simplifying and multiplying by 100%, represents the percent of students surveyed preferring baked potatoes to mashed potatoes.

2. $x + (x)(0.2) = \$120$

    $1.2x = 120$

    $x = 100$

    First set up an equation representing the total bill as two parts, money spent on food and a tip. The variable x represents the total spent on food. The tip is given by $0.2x$ as the tip is 20% of the money spent on food. Solving for x yields the amount of money spent strictly on food.

Exercise 5 (pg. 26)

1. Possible answers include but are not limited to:

    - Weather predictions

    - Test and class grades

    - Sports statistics or ratings

    - Shopping sales and discounts

    - Food labels and nutrition facts

Percents, Part 2

Exercise 1 (pg. 27)

1. **The correct answer is B.** 8% in its decimal form is 0.08. To find the percent of a number, multiply the percent in its decimal form by the number.

    60 · 0.08 = 4.8

2. **The correct answer is H.** 3% in its decimal form is 0.03. To find the percent of a number, multiply the percent in its decimal form by the original number.

    80 · 0.03 = 2.4

3. **The correct answer is D.** 125% in its decimal form is 1.25. To find the percent of a number, multiply the decimal form of the percent by the original number.

    40 · 1.25 = 50

Exercise 2 (pg. 28)

1. **The correct answer is D.** The children who are at least 8 years old are 8 years old or older, so add the percentages of children who are 8 years, 9 years, 10 years, and 11 years old together.

    14% + 15% + 17% + 12% = 58%

2. **The correct answer is F.** The number of students who chose "reading a book" is 3, and the total number of students surveyed is 40. Represented as a fraction, $\frac{3}{40}$ students chose "reading a book" out of the total students surveyed.

    Convert this value to a percentage: $\frac{3}{40}$ = 0.075 · 100% = 7.5%

3. **The correct answer is E.** The large triangle has been broken up into a total of 9 smaller triangles, of which 3 are shaded. Divide the number of shaded triangles by the total and convert the resulting decimal to a percentage in order to get the percentage of small triangles that are shaded.

    $3 \div 9 = 0.\overline{33} = 33\frac{1}{3}\%$

Exercise 3 (pg. 30)

1. Possible answers include but are not limited to the following:

    1) The most common method is to convert the percent to a decimal and multiply it by the number. 5% = 0.05, so 0.05 · N

    2) If you are more comfortable working with fractions, you can also convert 5% to a fraction and multiply. This works especially well if N will cancel (i.e. the denominator of the resulting fraction is a factor of N).

$5\% = \dfrac{5}{100} = \dfrac{1}{20}$ so $\dfrac{1}{20} \cdot N$

2. If Rhiannon surveyed 50 people, then each percentage can be converted to a decimal and multiplied by 50 in order to get the total number of people for each color.

Blue: 22% = 0.22 · 50 = 11
Red: 18% = 0.18 · 50 = 9
Purple: 18% = 0.18 · 50 = 9
Green: 14% = 0.14 · 50 = 7
Yellow: 12% = 0.12 · 50 = 6
Orange: 8% = 0.08 · 50 = 4
Pink: 6% = 0.06 · 50 = 3
Black: 2% = 0.02 · 50 = 1

Exercise 4 (pg. 32)

1. If the trapezoid is three times the size of the smaller triangle, then the larger triangle is 3 parts trapezoid and 1 part small triangle, for an overall total of 4 parts. This means the large triangle is $\dfrac{3}{4}$ trapezoid and $\dfrac{1}{4}$ small triangle. Since $\dfrac{3}{4} = 0.75 = 75\%$, the large triangle is 75% trapezoid.

2. If the value of *a* is equal to 3 times the value of *b*, then *a* = 3*b*. Therefore:

   10% of *a* is given by:

   10% · *a* = 0.10 · *a* = 0.10 · 3*b* = 0.30 · *b* = 30% · *b*

   10% of *a* is equal to 30% of *b*.

Exercise 5 (pg. 33)

1. Add up the percentages of each candy type.

   25 + 10 + 4 + 8 + 27 + 12 = 86

   Since 100% is a whole, subtract 86 from 100 to get the percentage of caramel candy and fruit chews combined.

   100 − 86 = 14%

   Since half (50%) of this amount is caramel candy and the other half is fruit chews, divide 14% by 2 to get the percentage of each.

   14 ÷ 2 = 7%

   (Students can also work a percentage calculation: 0.5(14) = 7%.)

   The candy jar is 7% caramel candies and 7% fruit chews.

Math Elements: Middle School Bell Ringers Teacher Manual

Percent Change

Exercise 1 (pg. 34)

1. **The correct answer is D.** Calculate 40% of $60 to determine by how much the printing cost increased. Then, add this to the original cost ($60).

   ($60)(0.40) = $24

   $24 + $60 = $84

2. **The correct answer is J.** Calculate 8% of $15. Then, add this value to the original price ($15).

   ($15)(0.08) + $15

   $1.20 + $15.00

   $16.20

3. **The correct answer is D.** Calculate $2\frac{1}{2}$% of $35,000.00. Then, add this to the original salary ($35,000.00).

   (0.025)($35,000.00) + $35,000.00

   $875 + $35,000.00 = $35,875.00

Exercise 2 (pg. 35)

1. **The correct answer is B.** Determine 25% of $74.96 to find out how much the lamp will be discounted, and then subtract this from the regular price ($74.96).

   $74.96 − (0.25)($74.96)

   $74.96 − $18.74

   $56.22

2. **The correct answer is J.** The price decreased by $15, so determine what percent of $60 this number represents.

   $\dfrac{60 - 45}{60} = \dfrac{15}{60} = \dfrac{1}{4} = 25\%$

3. **The correct answer is C.** The dress is discounted $10, so determine what percent of $40 this represents.

   $\dfrac{40 - 30}{40} = \dfrac{10}{40} = \dfrac{1}{4} = 25\%$

Exercise 3 (pg. 36)

1. The target office costs for next month are represented by this month's current cost minus 20% of this month's current costs.

   $550 − (0.20)($550)

   $550 − $110 = $440

2. To find the percent discount, find the difference between the two costs and determine what percent this represents of the original cost.

   $$\frac{250 - 175}{250} = \frac{75}{250} = \frac{3}{10} = 30\%$$

Exercise 4 (pg. 37)

1. Calculate 5% of $40,000, and then add this to the original salary.

   (0.05)($40,000) + $40,000

   $2,000 + $40,000

   $42,000

2. Calculate 15% of $45.40, and then subtract this from the original price to calculate the sale price.

   $45.40 − (0.15)($45.40)

   $45.40 − $6.81

   $38.59

Exercise 5 (pg. 38)

1. Answers will vary.

Math Elements: Middle School Bell Ringers Teacher Manual

Proportions

Exercise 1 (pg. 39)

1. **The correct answer is A.** Each serving is a total of 4 + 5 = 9 cups of juice. So, 4 cups of orange juice are needed for each 9 cups of juice. Set up a proportion and cross multiply to solve for the missing value:

   $$\frac{4}{9} = \frac{x}{90}$$

   $$x = \frac{(90)(4)}{9} = 40$$

   40 cups of orange juice are needed.

2. **The correct answer is G.** Set up a proportion to compare the dog size with the photo size.

   $$\frac{5}{14} = \frac{x}{23}$$

   $(23)(5) = 14x$

   $115 = 14x$

   $x = 8.21428571...$

   (Rounded to the nearest inch: 8 inches)

3. **The correct answer is B.** Set up a proportion and cross multiply to find the commission on the $900 purchase:

   $$\frac{36}{450} = \frac{x}{900}$$

   $$x = \frac{(36)(900)}{450}$$

   $x = 72$

   The commission is $72.

Exercise 2 (pg. 40)

1. **The correct answer is C.** Set up a proportion that compares the shadows of the tower and post with their heights.

   $\dfrac{4}{3} = \dfrac{x}{12}$

   $(12)(4) = 3x$

   $48 = 3x$

   $x = 16$

   The tower is 16 feet tall.

2. **The correct answer is J.** Set up a proportion that compares the width and length of the full-sized house with the model house and solve for the missing value.

   $\dfrac{16}{80} = \dfrac{x}{60}$

   $(60)(16) = 80x$

   $960 = 80x$

   $12 = x$

   The model is 12 inches wide.

3. **The correct answer is E.** Set up a proportion to solve for the missing number.

   $\dfrac{140}{x} = \dfrac{5}{14}$

   $5x = (140)(14)$

   $5x = 1960$

   $x = 392$

Exercise 3 (pg. 41)

1. The recipe calls for 2 cups of peanut butter per 5 cups of chocolate frosting ($\dfrac{2}{2+3} = \dfrac{2}{5}$). So to determine how many cups of peanut butter are needed, set up a proportion comparing the cups of peanut butter to cups of frosting and solve for the variable.

   $\dfrac{2}{5} = \dfrac{x}{30}$

   $(2)(30) = 5x$

60 = 5x

x = 12 cups of peanut butter needed

2. Instead of setting up a proportion, the student multiplied 210 by $\frac{3}{7}$.

   The student should have set up a proportion:

   $\frac{210}{x} = \frac{3}{7}$

   (210)(7) = 3x

   1,470 = 3x

   x = 490

Exercise 4 (pg. 43)

1. Set up a proportion to determine the length of the miniature model of the penguin.

   $\frac{8}{72} = \frac{x}{36}$

   (36)(8) = 72x

   288 = 72x

   x = 4

   The penguin model is 4 inches.

2. Set up a ratio to determine the waiter's tip on a $60 dinner:

   $\frac{9}{45} = \frac{x}{60}$

   (60)(9) = 45x

   540 = 45x

   x = 12

   The waiter's tip would be $12 on a $60 dinner.

Exercise 5 (pg. 44)

1. Create a proportion comparing the number of people to be served and the measurement for each ingredient.

   Solve for the new quantity for each ingredient.

   $$\frac{12 \text{ people}}{16 \text{ people}} = \frac{2 \text{ cups of flour}}{x \text{ cups of flour}}$$

   $x = 2\frac{2}{3}$ cups flour

   $$\frac{12 \text{ people}}{16 \text{ people}} = \frac{1.5 \text{ cups of white sugar}}{x \text{ cups of white sugar}}$$

   $x = 2$ cups white sugar

   $$\frac{12 \text{ people}}{16 \text{ people}} = \frac{0.5 \text{ cups of brown sugar}}{x \text{ cups of brown sugar}}$$

   $x = \frac{2}{3}$ cup brown sugar etc.

   New chocolate cake recipe for 16 people:

   $2\frac{2}{3}$ cups flour

   2 cups white sugar

   $\frac{2}{3}$ cups brown sugar

   $\frac{2}{3}$ cups cocoa powder

   $1\frac{1}{3}$ teaspoon vanilla extract

   $1\frac{1}{3}$ cup butter

   2 teaspoons salt

   4 eggs

   $1\frac{1}{3}$ cup milk

   2 teaspoons baking soda

   $2\frac{2}{3}$ teaspoons baking powder

Math Elements: Middle School Bell Ringers Teacher Manual

Polygon Area

Exercise 1 (pg. 45)

1. **The correct answer is C.** Multiply the length by the width to find the area of the square. This is shown by the expression 6 · 6.

2. **The correct answer is G.** Use the formula for the area of a rectangle to solve for the length.

    $A = l \cdot w$

    $112 = l \cdot 8$

    $\dfrac{112}{8} = l = 14$ inches

3. **The correct answer is D.** Use the formula for the area of a triangle to solve this problem.

    $A = \dfrac{1}{2} bh$

    $A = \dfrac{1}{2}(12)(10)$

    $A = 6 \cdot 10 = 60$ square feet

Exercise 2 (pg. 46)

1. **The correct answer is D.** Split the figure into two rectangles by drawing a vertical line. You now have a 6-foot-by-8-foot rectangle and a 10-foot-by-4-foot rectangle. Find the area of both rectangles and add them together to find the total area of the figure.

    6 · 8 = 48 square feet

    10 · 4 = 40 square feet

    48 + 40 = 88 total square feet

2. **The correct answer is H.** To find the area of the hexagon, count up the squares inside the figure. There are 18 full squares, 4 half-squares, 1 quarter-square and 1 three-quarter square. Add these pieces to get 21 square units.

3. **The correct answer is E.** This problem gives too much information. Simply use the side lengths of the square and disregard everything else. The square has side lengths that measure 7 centimeters. Because this is a square, its length and width are the same. Multiply length by width to find the area.

    $A = 7 \cdot 7 = 49$ square centimeters

Exercise 3 (pg. 48)

1. $A = \dfrac{1}{2} bh$

    $32 = \dfrac{1}{2}(8)h$

27

32 = 4h

h = 8 inches

2. Find the area of the square and the triangle and then add them together.

   Triangle:

   $A = \frac{1}{2}bh$

   $A = \frac{1}{2}(6)3$

   A = 3 · 3 = 9 square inches

   Square:

   A = l · w

   A = 6 · 6 = 36 square inches

   The area of the figure is 36 + 9 = 45 square inches.

Exercise 4 (pg. 50)

1. To find the area of the mirror, multiply the length by the width:

   30 · 46 = 1,380 square inches

2. First, find the length of the window by multiplying the width by 3:

   28 · 3 = 84 inches

   Now multiply the length by the width to find the area:

   28 · 84 = 2,352 square inches

Exercise 5 (pg. 51)

1. Answers will vary. Students may recognize that people buying or renting a home might have problems if they didn't know the square footage of the house. Others may describe needing to know what size picture to put in a picture frame, etc.

Ratios

Exercise 1 (pg. 52)

1. **The correct answer is C.** The ratio of cats to dogs is 18:63. Reduced, this is equivalent to $\frac{18}{9}:\frac{63}{9}$ = 2:7.

2. **The correct answer is H.** First, calculate the portion of the pizza that Jason ate.

   $1 - \frac{1}{3} - \frac{1}{4} = \frac{12}{12} - \frac{4}{12} - \frac{3}{12} = \frac{5}{12}$

   Compare the portions that each boy ate. The ratio is $\frac{4}{12}:\frac{3}{12}:\frac{5}{12}$, or 4:3:5.

3. **The correct answer is C.** Use the graph to find the number of students who selected cookie dough, 7, and the number of students who selected chocolate, 3. The ratio is thus 7:3.

Exercise 2 (pg. 53)

1. **The correct answer is B.** If the ratio of the model to the bridge is 1:18, then the ratio of each dimension should be 1:18 as well.

   $\frac{1}{18} = \frac{x}{126}$

   $126 = 18x$

   $x = 7$ feet long

   $\frac{1}{18} = \frac{x}{54}$

   $54 = 18x$

   $x = 3$ feet wide

   $\frac{1}{18} = \frac{x}{18}$

   $x = 1$ foot high

2. **The correct answer is J.** Use the graph to determine the percentage of those in the 25-35 year age bracket, 14, and then set this in a ratio with those not in the age bracket, 100 − 14 = 86. So the ratio is 14:86, or 7:43 when reduced.

3. **The correct answer is C.** Use the ratios with *y* to relate *x* and *z*.

   $\frac{x}{y} = \frac{2}{3}$ and $\frac{z}{y} = \frac{1}{4}$

   $\frac{x}{y} = \frac{8}{12}$ and $\frac{z}{y} = \frac{3}{12}$

   If *x*:*y* is 8:12 and *z*:*y* is 3:12, then the ratio of *x*:*z* is 8:3.

Exercise 3 (pg. 54)

1. The student gave the ratio of boys to girls. The ratio should be number of boys in the class:total number of students in the class.

    12:(15 +12)

    12:27

    4:9

2. The student did not convert the second ratio before relating *a* and *c*. The ratio of *b* to *c* can also be expressed as 7:21 (so *b* in this expression is equivalent to its value in the first ratio), so the ratio of *a* to *c* is 5:21.

Exercise 4 (pg. 55)

1. Use the chart to look up the values of the necessary percentages. The ratio of the number of neighbors who chose cat (17%) to the number who chose rabbit (8%) is 17:8.

2. Set up a ratio to solve for the missing value.

    $$\frac{1}{3} = \frac{15}{x}$$

    $x = (15)(3)$

    $x = 45$ miles

Exercise 5 (pg. 57)

1. Answers will vary.

Math Elements: Middle School Bell Ringers Teacher Manual

Exponents

Exercise 1 (pg. 58)

1. **The correct answer is D.** Multiply the coefficients: $2 \cdot 5 = 10$

   Then, multiply the variables by adding the exponents of similar variables: $y^{(3+7)} = y^{10}$

   $2y^3 \cdot 5y^7 = 10y^{10}$

2. **The correct answer is K.** When dividing variables with exponents, the exponents are subtracted from each other, leaving the result as the difference between the exponent of the numerator and the exponent of the denominator.

   $$\frac{4b^{2-6}}{4} = \frac{1b^{-4}}{1}$$

   The negative exponent can be changed to a positive exponent by moving the variable to the denominator.

   $$\frac{1}{b^4}$$

3. **The correct answer is E.** When exponents are raised to exponents, the resulting exponent of the variable is the product of the previous 2 exponents.

   $x^{8 \cdot 16} = x^{128}$

Exercise 2 (pg. 59)

1. **The correct answer is D.** First multiply the coefficients: $7 \cdot 14 = 98$

   Next multiply the variables by adding the exponents of the similar variables: $y^{(4+4)} = y^8$

   $7y^4 \cdot 14y^4 = 98y^8$

2. **The correct answer is K.** When exponents are divided, their values are subtracted from each other, leaving the result to be the difference between the numerator's exponent and the denominator's exponent.

   $x^{9-3} = x^6$

3. **The correct answer is A.** Raise both the coefficient and the variable to the -3 power:

   $2^{-3} = \dfrac{1}{2^3} = \dfrac{1}{8}$

   $(a^2)^{-3} = a^{-6} = \dfrac{1}{a^6}$

   Thus $\dfrac{1}{8} \cdot \dfrac{1}{a^6} = \dfrac{1}{8a^6}$

Exercise 3 (pg. 60)

1. When a power is raised to another power, the exponent is multiplied by the other exponent, not added. The answer is x^4 because $2 \cdot 2 = 4$, not because $2 + 2 = 4$. If the student were to keep trying addition, with $(x^2)^3$, for example, he or she would get x^{2+3} or x^5 instead of $x^{2 \cdot 3}$ or x^6, the correct answer.

2. When a term is divided by another term with the same coefficient, the coefficients do cancel out, but the exponents are subtracted, not reduced. The answer is $\frac{1}{x^2}$ because $2 - 4 = -2$. A negative exponent becomes positive when moved to the denominator, so x^{-2} becomes $\frac{1}{x^2}$.

Exercise 4 (pg. 61)

1. For exponents with the same base, simply add the exponents to arrive at the correct answer. Do not multiply the base by itself. 2^5 can be written as $2 \cdot 2 \cdot 2 \cdot 2 \cdot 2$, and 2^2 can be written as $2 \cdot 2$. Combine these terms to arrive at 2^7 or 128.

2. When adding like variables that are to the same power, the student must add the coefficients but not the exponents. Therefore, $2x^2 + 2x^2$ equals $4x^2$. Remember $x + x = 2x$ not x^2.

Exercise 5 (pg. 62)

1. Answers will vary. One such answer is the following:

$3^2 + 8^2 + 3^3 + (3x)^3 + 16y^3 + 10^2 + (x + 7)^4$

Math Elements: Middle School Bell Ringers Teacher Manual

Graphs and Charts: Word Problems

Exercise 1 (pg. 63)

1. **The correct answer is B.** Find the column containing the median of the data set. Since the median is the data point with eight data points on either side, the median is in the 61-70 column. The highest potential score in this column is 70.

2. **The correct answer is K.** Calculate 15% of the price of a long haircut, $45, and add the discounted haircut price to the cost of two full-price long haircuts.

   $45 + $45 + [$45 − (0.15 · $45)] =
   $90 + [$45 − $6.75] =
   $90 + $38.25 =
   $128.25

3. **The correct answer is D.** Add the data points between January 2015 and April 2015 and divide by 4.

   $9 + 17 + 22 + 29 = \frac{77}{4} = 19\frac{1}{4}$

Exercise 2 (pg. 65)

1. **The correct answer is B.** Calculate 3% of the price of gasoline in Year 5 and add this to that cost.

   (0.03 · $2.73) + $2.73 = $0.0819 + $2.73 = $2.8119 (rounded to the nearest $0.01 = $2.81)

2. **The correct answer is J.** Determine the ratio of the total shown in the graph to the total number of shirts ordered and use this ratio to calculate the number of green shirts ordered.

   $\frac{60}{600} = \frac{1}{10}$

   So, $\frac{12}{x} = \frac{1}{10}$

   x = 120 green shirts

3. **The correct answer is B.** Calculate the average by determining how many students studied each number of hours, adding them, and then dividing by 25.

   $\frac{0(2) + 1(4) + 2(5) + 3(7) + 4(4) + 5(3)}{25} =$

   $\frac{0 + 4 + 10 + 21 + 16 + 15}{25} = \frac{66}{25} = 2.64$ (rounded to the nearest tenth = 2.6)

Exercise 3 (pg. 67)

1. The student must take the average of the 20 data points represented by the graph, not the average of the four columns. Thus, the answer would be $\frac{0(4) + 1(6) + 2(7) + 3(3)}{20} = \frac{29}{20} = 1.45$.

2. The student must first calculate 5% of 280 (the number of mystery books sold in May) by multiplying 0.05 by 280 and then subtract this number from 280. Thus, the answer would be found by calculating 280 · 0.05, which yields 14, and 280 − 14, which yields 266.

Exercise 4 (pg. 69)

1. The price of a latte will be $3.54 because 20% of $2.95 is $0.59 and $0.59 + $2.95 = $3.54.

2. The average test score is the sum of the students' scores from February to May, divided by 4.

$$\frac{85 + 92 + 96 + 89}{4} = \frac{362}{4} = 90.5$$

Exercise 5 (pg. 71)

1. Answers will vary.

Math Elements: Middle School Bell Ringers Teacher Manual

Absolute Value

Exercise 1 (pg. 72)

1. **The correct answer is B.** Evaluate the absolute value, and then multiply by −3:

   $-3\,|-6+7| = -3 \cdot |1| = -3 \cdot 1 = -3$

2. **The correct answer is G.** Evaluate each absolute value, and then find the difference between the resulting values:

   $|10-7| - |3-7| =$

   $|3| - |-4| = 3 - 4 = -1$

3. **The correct answer is C.** Evaluate the absolute values, and then find the difference:

   $|9-4| - |4-9| =$

   $|5| - |-5| = 5 - 5 = 0$

Exercise 2 (pg. 73)

1. **The correct answer is D.** Evaluate the absolute values, and then find the difference:

   $|6-3| - |3-6| =$

   $|3| - |-3| = 3 - 3 = 0$

2. **The correct answer is H.** Evaluate the absolute values, and then find the difference:

   $|-5| - |8-27| =$

   $|-5| - |-19| =$

   $5 - 19 = -14$

3. **The correct answer is B.** Evaluate the absolute values, and then find the difference:

   $|9-4| - |1-7| =$

   $|5| - |-6| = 5 - 6 = -1$

Exercise 3 (pg. 74)

1. Evaluate the absolute value (absolute values are always positive). Then multiply by −6.

    $-6\,|-4-9| =$

    $-6\,|-13| =$

    $-6(13) = -78$

2. The absolute value represents a number's distance from zero. Both −4 and 4 are four units away from zero. This can easily be shown on a number line. Thus $|-4| = |4| = 4$.

Exercise 4 (pg. 75)

1. Evaluate the absolute value, and then multiply by −3:

    $-3\,|-1-4| = 5x$

    $-3\,|-5| = 5x$

    $-3(5) = 5x$

    $-15 = 5x$

    Divide both sides by 5 to find the value of x:

    $x = -3$

2. Evaluate the absolute values, and then add them together:

    $|4+3| + |-7-1| = 3x$

    $|7| + |-8| = 3x$

    $7 + 8 = 3x$

    $15 = 3x$

    Divide both sides by 3 to find the value of x:

    $15 = 3x$

    $x = 5$

    The student made the mistake of not taking the absolute value of −8, which made the left side of the equation equal to −1, when it should be equal to 15.

Exercise 5 (pg. 76)

1. His sister has traveled away 3 miles and back 2 miles, so she is 3 − 2 = 1 mile from home. His brother has traveled away 5 miles and back 1.5 miles, so he is 5 − 1.5 = 3.5 miles from home. Add their distances from home together to find out how far apart from each other they are. Mr. Young's brother and sister are 1 + 3.5 = 4.5 miles apart.

Inequalities

Exercise 1 (pg. 77)

1. **The correct answer is C.** Solve for p (remember to flip the inequality when dividing by a negative):

   $24 - 7p \leq 12$

   $-7p \leq -12$

   $p \geq \dfrac{12}{7}$

2. **The correct answer is H.** Solve for y (remember to flip the inequality when dividing by a negative):

   $6y + 3 < 6 + 9y$

   $-3y < 3$

   $y > -1$

3. **The correct answer is B.** Solve for q (remember to flip the inequality when dividing by a negative):

   $q - 8 < 8 + 9q$

   $-8q < 16$

   $q > -2$

Exercise 2 (pg. 78)

1. **The correct answer is B.** First, solve for u:

   $\dfrac{u}{5} + 7 < 8$

   $\dfrac{u}{5} < 1$

   $u < 5$

   The variable u is strictly less than and not equal to 5, so the greatest integer that satisfies the inequality is 4.

2. **The correct answer is K.** Solve for t (remember to flip the inequality when dividing by a negative):

   $5(t + 4) > 6(t - 10)$

   $5t + 20 > 6t - 60$

   $-t > -80$

   $t < 80$

3. **The correct answer is D.** Solve for z (remember to flip the inequality when dividing by a negative):

   $2(z + 10) < 3(z - 5)$

   $2z + 20 < 3z - 15$

   $-z < -35$

   $z > 35$

Exercise 3 (pg. 79)

1. The student mixes up the terms with variables with the terms without variables. He should consolidate like terms correctly.

   Consolidating the variable terms on the left-hand side gives $35s - 15s = 20s$.

   Consolidating constant terms on the right-hand side gives $-20 - 12 = -32$.

   Dividing both sides by 20 and simplifying the fraction gives $s > -\dfrac{32}{20} = -\dfrac{8}{5}$.

2. The student forgot to switch the direction of the inequality sign due to dividing both sides by a negative number.

   The correct answer is $p > -\dfrac{13}{4}$.

Exercise 4 (pg. 81)

1. First, solve for x (remember to flip the inequality when dividing by a negative):

   $12 < 14x + \dfrac{6}{23}$

   $12 - \dfrac{6}{23} < 14x$

   $\dfrac{270}{23} < 14x$

   $\dfrac{270}{(23)(14)} < x$

   $\dfrac{135}{161} < x$

   The fraction $\dfrac{135}{161}$ is less than 1, and x must be greater than the fraction. Thus, the lowest possible integer value of x satisfying the inequality is 1.

2. Solve for k:

   $33k - 5 > 6$

   $33k > 11$

   $k > \dfrac{11}{33}$

   $k > \dfrac{1}{3}$

Exercise 5 (pg. 82)

1. greater than, less than, equal to

   They are symbols used in inequalities. They describe the different relationships between expressions on either side of the symbol.

Math Elements: Middle School Bell Ringers Teacher Manual

Sequences

Exercise 1 (pg. 83)

1. **The correct answer is C.** The geometric sequence defined above has a starting term of 2 and a common ratio of 1.5. Multiply 4.5 by 1.5 to get 6.75.

2. **The correct answer is G.** The geometric sequence defined above has a starting term of 3 and a common ratio of 3; equivalently, the first term is 3^1 and the fifth term is 3^5. Therefore, the second term of the sequence is $3^2 = 9$.

3. **The correct answer is D.** Set up an arithmetic sequence to solve this problem. Let −3 be the first term of the sequence. −3, __, a, 9, __, __, 21

    Find the common difference of the sequence by subtracting 9 from 21 and dividing by 3.

    21 − 9 = 12

    12 ÷ 3 = 4

    Since you know the common difference to be 4, subtract 4 from 9 to get the value of a.

    9 − 4 = 5

Exercise 2 (pg. 84)

1. **The correct answer is A.** The geometric sequence defined above has first term −0.425 and a common ratio of −3. Multiply the fifth term in the sequence by −3 to find the sixth term.

    −34.425 · −3 = 103.275

2. **The correct answer is F.** Find the common difference of the sequence by subtracting 9 from 20 and dividing by 4.

    20 − 9 = 11

    11 ÷ 4 = 2.75

    Since the common difference of the arithmetic sequence defined above is 2.75, the first 3 terms are 0.75, 3.50, and 6.25. Add these together to get 10.5.

3. **The correct answer is D.** The geometric sequence defined above has a common ratio of $-\frac{1}{4}$. Thus, the fourth term may be found by dividing −3 by −4.

    $-3 \div -4 = \frac{3}{4}$

Exercise 3 (pg. 85)

1. Because the sequence above is geometric, it must have a common ratio, namely 4, which dictates that the fourth term in the sequence is $4^4 = 256$.

2. Bertha is incorrect because the above sequence is arithmetic, with a first term of 14 and a common difference of 14.

Exercise 4 (pg. 86)

1. Find the common difference of the sequence by subtracting 6 from 8 and dividing by 4.

   $8 - 6 = 2$

   $2 \div 4 = 0.5$

   The common difference of the arithmetic series above is 0.5, so

   $a_3 = 6 - 0.5 = 5.5$

   $a_2 = 5.5 - 0.5 = 5$

   $a_1 = 5 - 0.5 = 4.5$

   and

   $a_3 + a_2 + a_1 = 5.5 + 5 + 4.5 = 15$

2. Sean is incorrect because he has found the 5th and 6th terms, respectively. The common ratio of the geometric sequence above is 2, so the 6th and 7th terms would be 64 and 128, respectively.

Exercise 5 (pg. 87)

1. 1, 3, 5, 7, 9, 11 (Add 2 to each term.)

   2, 6, 18, 54, 162, 486 (Multiply each term by 3.)

   12, 18, 30, 54, 102, 198 (Add 6 to the first term. Then add 12 (twice 6) to the next term. Then add 24 (twice 12). Then add 48 (twice 24), etc.

   $x, x^2, x^3, x^4, x^5, x^6$ (Each term is multiplied by x.)

   $x, 2x^3, 4x^5, 8x^7, 16x^9, 32x^{11}$ (Each term is multiplied by $2x^2$.)

Substitution

Exercise 1 (pg. 88)

1. **The correct answer is E.** Plug the values for *a*, *b*, and *c* into the expression given:

   $ab - bc =$

   $(4)(6) - (6)(-3) =$

   $(24) - (-18) =$

   $24 + 18 = 42$

2. **The correct answer is F.** Plug the values for *a*, *b*, and *c* into the expression given:

   $(c + b - a)(a + c) =$

   $(6 + 9 - (-7))((-7) + 6) =$

   $(15 + 7)(-7 + 6) =$

   $(22)(-1) = -22$

3. **The correct answer is A.** Plug the values for *a*, *b*, and *c* into the expression given:

   $(c + b - a)(a + c) =$

   $(7 + 3 - (-8))((-8) + 7) =$

   $(10 + 8)(-8 + 7) =$

   $(18)(-1) = -18$

Exercise 2 (pg. 89)

1. **The correct answer is A.** Plug the values for *x*, *y*, and *z* into the expression given:

   $(x + y - z)(x + z) =$

   $(1 + 6 - (-4))(1 + (-4)) =$

   $(7 + 4)(1 - 4) =$

   $(11)(-3) = -33$

2. **The correct answer is H.** Plug the values for x, y, and z into the expression given:

$$xyz + \frac{x+z}{2y} + x =$$

$$(1)(2)(3) + \frac{1+3}{2(2)} + 1 =$$

$$6 + \frac{4}{4} + 1 =$$

$$6 + 1 + 1 = 8$$

3. **The correct answer is A.** Plug the values for x, y, and z into the expression given:

$$(x + y - z)(y + z) =$$

$$(2 + 5 - (-8))(5 + (-8)) =$$

$$(7 + 8)(5 - 8) =$$

$$(15)(-3) = -45$$

Exercise 3 (pg. 90)

1. Plug the values for p, q, and r into the expression given:

$$6p^2 - qr =$$

$$6(2)^2 - (8)(3) =$$

$$6(4) - 24 =$$

$$24 - 24 = 0$$

2. Plug the values for a, b, c, and d into the expression given:

$$\frac{a}{b} + x = \frac{c}{d}$$

$$\frac{8}{4} + x = \frac{9}{3}$$

$$2 + x = 3$$

$$x = 1$$

Exercise 4 (pg. 91)

1. Remember that a negative multiplied by another negative is a positive, and a positive multiplied by a negative is a negative. This means that an odd number of multiplied negatives will give a negative answer, and an even number of multiplied negatives will give a positive answer. This problem involves multiplying three negative numbers, so the answer should be negative:

    $xyz = (-2)(-5)(-4) =$

    $(10)(-4) = -40$

2. The student forgot the negative sign of *y*. After the values are plugged in, the equation should look like this:

    $4 - 2(-3) + (-7) =$

    $4 - (-6) - 7 =$

    $4 + 6 - 7 = 3$

Exercise 5 (pg. 92)

1. Create a system of equations:

    $c = 2d + 1$

    $c + d = 22$

    Substitute the first equation into the second.

    $2d + 1 + d = 22$

    $3d + 1 = 22$

    $3d = 21$

    $d = 7$

    Substitute *d* back in to one of the original equations to solve for *c*.

    $c + 7 = 22$

    $c = 15$

    Mrs. Kerry has 7 dogs and 15 cats.

# Linear Equations

Exercise 1 (pg. 93)

1. **The correct answer is B.** Find the slope of the line and use the point-slope formula to then determine the equation in slope-intercept form.

    $$m = \frac{5 - (-3)}{4 - 2} = \frac{8}{2} = 4$$

    $$y - 5 = 4(x - 4)$$

    $$y - 5 = 4x - 16$$

    $$y = 4x - 11$$

2. **The correct answer is F.** Determine the slope and then use the point-slope form to transform the equation into slope-intercept form.

    $$m = \frac{-4 - (-9)}{8 - (-7)} = \frac{5}{15} = \frac{1}{3}$$

    $$y + 4 = \frac{1}{3}(x - 8)$$

    $$y + 4 = \frac{1}{3}x - \frac{8}{3}$$

    $$y = \frac{1}{3}x - \frac{20}{3}$$

3. **The correct answer is B.** Determine the slope. Since the line passes through the origin, the *y*-intercept is 0.

    $$m = \frac{-5 - 0}{10 - 0} = -\frac{5}{10} = -\frac{1}{2}$$

    $$y = -\frac{1}{2}x$$

Exercise 2 (pg. 94)

1. **The correct answer is C.** Find the slope and the use one of the known points and the point-intercept form to convert the equation into slope-intercept form.

   $m = \dfrac{1-4}{4-(-2)} = \dfrac{-3}{6} = -\dfrac{1}{2}$

   $y - 1 = -\dfrac{1}{2}(x - 4)$

   $y - 1 = -\dfrac{1}{2}x + 2$

   $y = -\dfrac{1}{2}x + 3$

   The y-intercept is 3.

2. **The correct answer is K.** The y-intercept is between 8 and 10, so only $y = 3x + 9$ can be correct (as all equations are written in slope-intercept form).

3. **The correct answer is D.** Find the slope and then use one of the known points and the point-intercept form to convert the equation into slope-intercept form.

   $m = \dfrac{3 - 11}{0 - (-4)} = \dfrac{-8}{4} = -2$

   $y - 3 = -2(x - 0)$

   $y - 3 = -2x$

   $y = -2x + 3$

Exercise 3 (pg. 95)

1. The student found the incorrect slope. Slope should be calculated with the "rise over run" formula, with the y values in the numerator and the x values in the denominator.

   Slope: $\dfrac{11 - 2}{3 - 0} = \dfrac{9}{3} = 3$

   Since a point on the line is (0,2), the y-intercept is 2.

   $y = 3x + 2$

2. The student incorrectly substituted in the *y* and *x* values into the equation. The correct answer should be the following:

$y = mx + b$

$7 = m(1) + b$

$7 = \dfrac{7 - (-1)}{1 - (-3)}(1) + b$

$7 = 2(1) + b$

$7 = 2 + b$

$5 = b$

Exercise 4 (pg. 97)

1. The slope-intercept form is $y = mx + b$. The *y*-intercept is known to be 6, so calculate the slope.

   $m = \dfrac{6 - 4}{0 - (-2)} = \dfrac{2}{2} = 1$

   $y = x + 6$

2. Determine the equation, in slope-intercept form, that represents the line.

   $m = \dfrac{5 - 4}{2 - 3} = \dfrac{1}{-1} = -1$

   $y = mx + b$

   $5 = (-1)(2) + b$

   $5 = -2 + b$

   $7 = b$

   The *y*-intercept is 7.

Exercise 5 (pg. 98)

1. straight line, linear, first power

   A straight line is the graph of a linear equation. A linear equation has a variable to the first power and no higher power.

Modeling Equations: Word Problems

Exercise 1 (pg. 99)

1. **The correct answer is C.** If *y* represents the distance traveled per hour, then *y* must be multiplied by 4 hours to yield the number of miles traveled, 4*y*.

2. **The correct answer is F.** Simplify 3(2*x* + 1) to 6*x* + 3. The correct answer will thus contain six circles and three triangles.

3. **The correct answer is E.** Translate the verbal expression into mathematical terms. "*x* squared" is x^2, and "25 more than the product of 5 and *x*" is represented by 25 + 5*x*.

Exercise 2 (pg. 100)

1. **The correct answer is D.** For one month, the total costs will be represented by the fixed costs ($20,000) plus the cost of the candles produced that month (*x* · $0.80) or the following:

   $20,000 + $0.80*x*

2. **The correct answer is J.** The total amount is given by the cost of nonmember tickets multiplied by the number of nonmember tickets sold plus the cost of member tickets multiplied by the number of member tickets sold. Therefore, the total cost is expressed by the following:

   28 · *n* + 20 · 45

   28*n* + 20(45)

3. **The correct answer is E.** Use the average formula and plug in the known values.

   $$\frac{\text{Sum of speeds at each hour}}{\text{Number of hours}} = \text{Average speed in mph}$$

   $$\frac{6x + 5(455)}{11} = 400$$

   6*x* + 5(455) = 11(400)

Exercise 3 (pg. 101)

1. The student has incorrectly placed the 5 in his or her expression, since 15*x* is 5 more than $7x^3$.

   $15x = 5 + 7x^3$

2. The total amount earned will be the price of cookies times the number of cookies sold plus the price of brownies times the number of brownies sold.

   ($2.50)(137) + $3.25*x*

Exercise 4 (pg. 103)

1. Multiply the man's speed by the number of hours traveled.

   35 miles per hour · x hours

   $35x$ miles

2. Total revenue will be represented by the cost of a student ticket multiplied by the number of student tickets sold plus the cost of an adult ticket multiplied by the number of adult tickets sold.

   $6(245) + 9y$

Exercise 5 (pg. 104)

1. You could model this scenario by the equation $h = 3c + 5$, in which h is the number of homework problems and c is the number of classwork problems. The main benefit of creating an equation is that it allows you to solve for the number of problems quickly.

Solving Equations: Word Problems

Exercise 1 (pg. 105)

1. **The correct answer is A.** Write the equation for each difficulty. Set the two equations equal to each other. Then, solve for the variable.

   $y = 45x + 175$

   $y = 75x + 25$

   $45x + 175 = 75x + 25$

   $30x = 150$

   $x = 5$

2. **The correct answer is G.** Solve the equation for F, then plug the outside temperature in for C.

   $C = \frac{5}{9}(F - 32)$

   $F = \frac{9}{5}C + 32$

   $F = \frac{9}{5}5 + 32$

   $F = 41$

3. **The correct answer is C.** Write down the equation. Then, solve for x and $x + 2$.

   $x + 4(x + 2) = 43$

   $5x + 8 = 43$

   $5x = 35$

   $x = 7$

   $x + 2 = 9$

Exercise 2 (pg. 106)

1. **The correct answer is D.** Solve the equation for h then plug in the volume, length, and width.

   $V = \dfrac{lwh}{3}$

   $h = \dfrac{3V}{lw}$

   $h = \dfrac{3 \cdot 56}{4 \cdot 6}$

   $h = 7$

2. **The correct answer is J.** Write an expression in terms of the value of each coin in pennies then solve for the number of dimes.

   Pennies: $(0.01)(p)$

   Nickles: $(0.05)(3p)$

   Dimes: $(0.10)(p - 2)$

   Quarters: $(0.25)(p + 1)$

   $p + n + d + q = \$6.17$

   Plug the expressions for each coin into the equation above.

   $(0.01)p + (0.05)(3p) + (0.10)(p - 2) + (0.25)(p + 1) = 6.17$

   $0.01p + 0.15p + 0.10p - 0.20 + 0.25p + 0.25 = 6.17$

   $0.51p = 6.12$

   $p = 12$

   Since Gerald found 12 pennies and there were 2 fewer dimes than pennies, he must have found $12 - 2 = 10$ dimes.

3. **The correct answer is C.** Plug in the answer options to find which one would yield the area given in the question. Remember that the formula for area of a rectangle is $A = lw$. In this case, length is referred to in the question as how tall the rectangle is.

   Always begin with the middle option, choice C. Let length be one third of the width you plug in, since the rectangle is three times as wide as it is tall. $A = 54 \cdot \frac{1}{3}(54)$

$A = 54 \cdot 18$

$A = 972$

In this case, the first answer option tried is correct. The length is 18 inches and the width is 54 inches.

Exercise 3 (pg. 107)

1. Abigail's mistake is that she is distributing the $\frac{9}{5}$ across C and 32 when it should only be multiplied by C. The correct formula is $F = \frac{9}{5} C + 32$.

2. The mistake the student made is using $x + 1$ as the second integer. If x is an even integer, the next consecutive even integer will be $x + 2$. Otherwise, the answer the student will arrive at will be an even number and an odd number, which is incorrect.

Exercise 4 (pg. 109)

1. The expression needed is $\frac{x}{2} + 4(x + 1) = 58$.

    $x + 8(x + 1) = 116$

    $9x + 8 = 116$

    $9x = 108$

    $x = 12$

    $x + 1 = 13$

2. Justin could use the expression $C = 15N + 59$ where C is his total cost and N is the number of months he has played. At a year and a half, he will have paid $15 \cdot 18 + 59 = \$329$.

Exercise 5 (pg. 111)

1. Answers will vary.

Math Elements: Middle School Bell Ringers Teacher Manual

Average, Median, and Mode, Part 1

Exercise 1 (pg. 112)

1. **The correct answer is D.** Add the numbers in the list together. Then, divide by how many numbers there are.

    $$\frac{52 + 64 + 61 + 22 + 35 + 54 + 31 + 41 + 64 + 26}{10} = \frac{450}{10} = 45$$

2. **The correct answer is J.** Add the numbers together. Then, divide by how many numbers there are.

    $$\frac{7 + 8 + 8}{3} = \frac{23}{3} = 7\frac{2}{3}$$

3. **The correct answer is D.** Place the numbers in order from least to greatest. Then, find the middle number.

    12, 12, 13, <u>14</u>, 28, 37, 43

    The median is 14.

Exercise 2 (pg. 113)

1. **The correct answer is B.** Place the numbers in order from least to greatest. Then, find the middle number.

    47, 54, 66, 67, <u>68</u>, 75, 82, 82, 89

2. **The correct answer is H.** Subtract the smallest score from the largest score for each team. Then, choose the one with the smallest difference.

    Team A: 50 − 32 = 18

    Team B: 48 − 42 = 6

    Team C: 47 − 25 = 22

3. **The correct answer is B.** Add up the prices from each year. Then, divide by the number of years.

    $$\frac{\$4.64 + \$4.70 + \$4.70 + \$4.57 + \$4.55}{5} = \frac{\$23.16}{5} = \$4.63$$

Exercise 3 (pg. 115)

1. Though James arrived at the correct answer, he found the mean rather than the median. This will not always work if the set of numbers is different.

    To solve for the median, place the numbers in order from least to greatest and find the middle number.

    107, 118, 122, 127, <u>127</u>, 127, 133, 135, 147

2. Although the student has arrived at the correct answer, she has actually found the median value. To find the mode, the student should determine which value shows up most often in the set. The student's mistaken method would not have worked if the numbers were different or if there were a different amount of numbers.

Exercise 4 (pg. 117)

1. The range Bryan is interested in knowing is 39. Range is the largest number minus the smallest number in a group, and 46 − 7 = 39.

2. The student's average science exam grade is 72. The average of a set of numbers is found by adding the numbers together and dividing by how many numbers there are.

$$\frac{87 + 33 + 76 + 94 + 70}{5} = \frac{360}{5} = 72$$

Exercise 5 (pg. 119)

1. Mean, range, median, and mode.

   These are all terms used to describe a set of data.

   Mean: A calculation of the center of a set of data found by dividing the sum of the data items in a set by the total number of data items.

   Median: The middle data item in a set.

   Mode: The number that appears most often in a data set.

   Range: The difference between the largest number and the smallest number in a data set.

Average, Median, and Mode, Part 2

Exercise 1 (pg. 120)

1. **The correct answer is D.** Add the number enrolled in each section of Biology 1 and divide by the number of sections.

   $$\frac{33 + 24 + 33}{3} = \frac{90}{3} = 30 = \frac{90}{3} = 30$$

2. **The correct answer is J.** Add the numbers together and divide by how many numbers there are.

   $$\frac{285 + 264 + 277 + 214 + 290}{5} = \frac{1{,}330}{5} = 266$$

3. **The correct answer is C.** Add the numbers together. Then, divide by how many numbers there are.

   $$\frac{(-2) + (-1) + 0 + 2 + (-4) + 3 + 3 + 0 + (-1)}{9} = \frac{0}{9} = 0$$

Exercise 2 (pg. 121)

1. **The correct answer is E.** Divide the sum by the number of participants.

   $$\frac{118.4}{8} = 14.8$$

2. **The correct answer is H.** Drop the lowest score. Add the remaining scores and divide by the number of scores being used.

   $$\frac{56 + 61 + 65 + 70}{4} = \frac{252}{4} = 63.0$$

3. **The correct answer is B.** Place the numbers in order from least to greatest and find the middle number.

   −12, −9, − 7, −6, 3, 7, 8

Exercise 3 (pg. 122)

1. There are 6 total games being averaged not 2. His calculation should be the following:

   $$\frac{252 + 215 + 290 + 237 + 281 + x}{6} = 260$$

   $1{,}275 + x = 1{,}560$

   $x = 285$

   Gerald needs to score 285 in his next game.

2. Although Jonathan dropped the lowest test grade from his total, he averaged as if the grade included 5 exams rather than 4. His procedure will not work since he should only be considering 4 exams. The sum of his test scores should be divided by 4, not 5.

Exercise 4 (pg. 124)

1. Samantha will need a total of 7 and one half cups of flour. Since the average amount of flour needed per recipe is 1.5 cups and she would like to try 5 recipes, she will need 1.5 · 5 = 7.5 cups.

2. The median value is 78. The median value of a set of numbers is found by ordering the numbers from least to greatest, then locating the number in the middle.

   39, 41, 63, 63, 64, <u>78</u>, 78, 115, 216, 285, 312

Exercise 5 (pg. 126)

1. Calculate the averages by adding up the scores and dividing by the number of scores, 10.

   Best Friend average = 7.1 (winner)

   Arch Nemesis average = 6.4

   For the bonus, remove the highest and lowest numbers from each person's scores and recalculate the average. Divide by 8 this time instead of 10.

   Best Friend average = 7.25 (winner)

   Arch Nemesis average = 6.375

Math Elements: Middle School Bell Ringers Teacher Manual

Counting

Exercise 1 (pg. 127)

1. **The correct answer is D.** Draw out the diagonals and count them. Be sure not to count repeated diagonals coming from opposite vertices. The first and second vertices will both have 5 diagonals coming from them for a total of 10 diagonals.

   The third vertex will have 4 new diagonals coming from it.

   The fourth vertex will have 3 new diagonals coming from it.

   The fifth vertex will have 2 new diagonals coming from it.

   The sixth vertex will have 1 new diagonal coming from it.

   The seventh and eighth vertices will already have all possible diagonals drawn to connect them to other vertices and will therefore have 0 new diagonals beginning from them. Add the total number of diagonals drawn: 10 + 4 + 3 + 2 + 1 + 0 = 20 unique diagonals.

2. **The correct answer is K.** Use the largest coins possible. One 50¢ coin, four 5¢ coins, and three 1¢ coins give 73¢.

   50 + 4(5) + 3(1) = 50 + 20 + 3 = 73

3. **The correct answer is B.** Write out the whole numbers from 131 through 147 and count the ones whose ones digit is less than the tens digit:

   131, 132, 133, 134, 135, 136, 137, 138, 139, 140, 141, 142, 143, 144, 145, 146, 147

   The numbers with a ones digit less than the tens digit are 131, 132, 140, 141, 142, 143.

Exercise 2 (pg. 128)

1. **The correct answer is C.** Starting with the largest quantity, add as many as possible before moving to the next smaller amount. Multiply the costs of each sized box by the quantities purchased and add the prices together.

   2 · $4.95 + $2.25 + 3 · $0.45 = $13.50

2. **The correct answer is H.** Draw out each table and put a person in each one so that none are empty. Then, fill each table up to 6 people until no more can be filled. You will have 3 tables with 6 people, 5 tables with 1 person, and 4 remaining. These four can be divided up in any way among the remaining 5 tables that are not full, but they cannot make another completely full table. So the correct answer is 3 full tables.

3. **The correct answer is D.** Add each answer choice to the numerator and denominator then reduce.

   8 + 2 = 10

   13 + 2 = 15

   $\frac{10}{15} = \frac{2}{3}$

Exercise 3 (pg. 129)

1. There are 5 distinct diagonals. The student did not take into account that the same diagonal can be drawn from 2 different vertices. The student should divide her answer in half to avoid counting diagonals twice.

2. Brandon incorrectly added a whole number to the numerator and denominator independently. First, Brandon should have found a common denominator.

$$\frac{-8}{1} + \frac{9}{12} = \frac{-96}{12} + \frac{9}{12} =$$

$$\frac{-87}{12} = \frac{-29}{4}$$

Exercise 4 (pg. 130)

1. George is able to completely fill 7 of his dinner tables. After ensuring that no table is empty, there will be 28 people left to seat. Since each table needs 4 more people to be filled, he is able to fill 7 tables before not having enough people left to seat.

2. Jeffery will need 20 lengths of rope. Since an octagon has 8 corners and since only 5 diagonals can be run from any corner, 8 · 5 = 40. Since this is including every diagonal twice, Jeffery needs to divide by 2 to get a total of 20 lengths of rope.

Exercise 5 (pg. 131)

1. Because 7 8 9. When said aloud, 8 sounds like "ate." The number 7 ate the number 9. So 6 is afraid for his life!

Math Elements: Middle School Bell Ringers Teacher Manual

Probability, Part 1

Exercise 1 (pg. 132)

1. **The correct answer is C.** Divide the number of pink marbles by the total number of marbles.

   The probability that the marble is pink is $\frac{7}{15}$.

2. **The correct answer is J.** Add the number of cars and airplanes. Then, divide by the total number of toys.

   $$\frac{9+3}{30} = \frac{12}{30} = \frac{2}{5}$$

3. **The correct answer is B.** Add the number of orange and yellow marbles. Then, divide by the total number of marbles.

   $$\frac{3+9}{36} = \frac{12}{36} = \frac{1}{3}$$

Exercise 2 (pg. 134)

1. **The correct answer is E.** Add the number of beans that aren't lima beans. Then, divide by the total number of beans.

   $$\frac{13+5}{24} = \frac{18}{24} = \frac{3}{4}$$

2. **The correct answer is H.** Divide the number of black marbles by the total number of marbles. $\frac{4}{16} = \frac{1}{4}$

3. **The correct answer is D.** Add up the number of candies that are not banana. Then, divide by the total number of candies.

   $$\frac{48+92}{200} = \frac{140}{200} = \frac{7}{10}$$

Exercise 3 (pg. 135)

1. Although Jerry is correct that any particular marble has a $\frac{1}{16}$ chance of being chosen at random, he must consider the fact that he has more than 1 of some color marbles, which increases the chance of selecting that particular color. He actually has $\frac{2}{16}$ chance of randomly selecting a pink marble.

2. Ryan has actually written down the chance that he WILL select an orange piece. To find the chance that he will NOT select an orange, he should subtract the chance of drawing an orange piece from 1.

   $$1 - \frac{11}{50} = \frac{39}{50}$$

Exercise 4 (pg. 137)

1. Jimmy has a $\frac{28}{100}$ chance of selecting a nougat candy from the bag because, of the 100 total candies in the bag, 28 of them are nougat.

2. There is a $\frac{23}{25}$ chance that neither Scott nor Tasha will be chosen to run this round. Each child has a $\frac{1}{25}$ chance of being chosen, so $\frac{25-2}{25} = \frac{23}{25}$.

Exercise 5 (pg. 138)

1. The chance that it is currently raining with winds above 20 mph is 18%. This is because there is a 90% chance that it is raining and a 20% chance that the wind is above 20 mph. So to find the probability of them happening simultaneously, multiply the two percentages together:

   $0.9 \cdot 0.2 = 0.18$ or 18%.

   The chance that it will hail tomorrow with winds below 20 mph is 20.25%. This is because there is a 45% chance that it will hail tomorrow and a 100% − 55% = 45% chance that the wind will be below 20 mph tomorrow. So to find the probability of them happening simultaneously, multiply the two percentages together:

   $0.45 \cdot 0.45 = 0.2025$ or 20.25%.

Math Elements: Middle School Bell Ringers Teacher Manual

Probability, Part 2

Exercise 1 (pg. 139)

1. **The correct answer is E.** Probabilities must be between 0 and 1.

2. **The correct answer is F.** Multiply the probability of rolling 1 by itself. $\frac{1}{8} \cdot \frac{1}{8} = \frac{1}{64}$

3. **The correct answer is C.** Divide the number of green sections by the total number of sections.

Exercise 2 (pg. 141)

1. **The correct answer is C.** Since only 20 members of the club are eligible to be chosen, the probability of anyone being chosen is $\frac{1}{20}$.

2. **The correct answer is H.** Divide each possible point value by 2 and 3 to see how many are multiples of both 2 and 3. Then divide the number that are divisible by the total number of possibilities.

   The numbers 18, 30, 54, and 6 are all divisible by both 2 and 3. There are a total of 9 numbers, so the probability is $\frac{4}{9}$.

3. **The correct answer is B.** Divide the number of times the player scored 13 assists by the total number of games. Since the second row has 1 and 3 as a stem-leaf combination twice, there are 2 instances of a 13-assist game. So, the probability that the hockey player scored 13 assists in a game is $\frac{2}{13}$.

Exercise 3 (pg. 143)

1. The student must have made a mistake because $\frac{7}{30} + \frac{13}{30} + \frac{4}{30} + \frac{10}{30} = \frac{34}{30}$, and probabilities must be between 0 and 1, not greater than 1.

2. Joey's mistake was adding 2 to his individual likelihood of being selected rather than subtracting 2 from the total number of possible choices. Joey's actual chance of being selected is $\frac{1}{10}$.

Exercise 4 (pg. 145)

1. There is a $\frac{1}{400}$ chance that Jessica will score a critical hit on her next roll. The chance of rolling a 20 on an individual 20-sided die is $\frac{1}{20}$. Since she must roll doubles, the odds of the two dice are multiplied together.

   $\frac{1}{20} \cdot \frac{1}{20} = \frac{1}{400}$

2. There is a $\frac{1}{14}$ chance that the horror movie will be chosen. Though there are initially 20 movies, when the 6 science fiction movies are eliminated, there are only 14 movies left to choose from.

Exercise 5 (pg. 146)

1. Answers will vary. Mutually exclusive events in probability are outcomes or actions that cannot both happen or cannot happen at the same time.

Math Elements: Middle School Bell Ringers Teacher Manual

Data Interpretation

Exercise 1 (pg. 147)

1. **The correct answer is E.** Add up the changes in depth for each hour during the time interval.

   50 + 0 + 250 + 150 = 450 meters

2. **The correct answer is H.** Examine the time values on the *x*-axis when the line is at or above 300 meters. The submersible first reaches 300 meters at about 10:30 and stays at or below 300 meters until about 1:30. From 10:30 to 1:30 is 3 hours and 0 minutes.

3. **The correct answer is B.** Observe the motion from the graph, remembering that an increased depth is descending.

Exercise 2 (pg. 150)

1. **The correct answer is B.** Subtract the number of testers that only requested one type of game from the total number of testers.

   220 − 73 − 41 − 68 = 38 game testers

2. **The correct answer is H.** Divide the number of chickens born at Chirptown by the total number of chickens represented in the figure. $\frac{450}{1,500} = \frac{3}{10}$

3. **The correct answer is B.** The population begins increasing quickly before the predator causes the rate of reproduction to slow down. The population continues to increase, but at a slower rate.

Exercise 3 (pg. 153)

1. Although Dustin is correct that the object is traveling more quickly from 7:00 A.M. to 8:00 A.M. than from 8:00 A.M. to 9:00 A.M., he has ignored that the graph is reporting depth, meaning the object is descending rather than ascending. His reasoning will only work if the object is ascending.

2. Even though the object ended only 100 m from the starting position, it traveled more than 100 m to reach that position. The object first travels a distance of 250 m in the first hour and then traveled an additional 150 m in the second hour to reach its final position. Even though the travel is in opposite directions, it still adds to the total distance traveled. The object traveled a total of 250 + 150 = 400 m.

Exercise 4 (pg. 155)

1. 38 people preferred at most 2 of the superheroes. To determine this, add up the total number of people and subtract the number that preferred all 3 superheroes.

   7 + 11 + 6 + 5 + 3 + 6 + 2 = 40 people

   40 − 2 = 38 people

2. Brittany can travel 8,900 m more before she needs to change the oil.

   Add up how far the submersible traveled each hour.

   50 + 100 + 50 + 0 + 250 + 150 + 100 + 400 = 1,100 m

   Over the course of her trip, she traveled a total of 1,100 m. Subtract this amount from 10,000 m.

   10,000 m − 1,100 m = 8,900 m

Exercise 5 (pg. 157)

1. You can answer question 3. It refers only to states in the chart and all you need to know is the total population, which is given in the chart, to answer the questions. If every state is split evenly between men and women, California would have the most women.

   You can also answer question 4, because you are given the population of the states. Georgia, Ohio, Pennsylvania, Illinois, New York, Florida, Texas, and California all have a population higher than 10,000,000.

   The other questions refer to details that are not given in the table. Therefore, no conclusion can be made about them.

Math Elements: Middle School Bell Ringers Teacher Manual

Factors, Part 1

Exercise 1 (pg. 158)

1. **The correct answer is E.** Divide 12 by all of the integers smaller than or equal to it, until you have exhausted all possible values.

    12 ÷ 1 = 12

    12 ÷ 2 = 6

    12 ÷ 3 = 4

    So, the list is 1, 2, 3, 4, 6, and 12.

2. **The correct answer is G.** Divide 84 by each of the choices:
    84 ÷ 9 = 9.3. (not a factor, quotient is not a whole number)

3. **The correct answer is C.** Divide 50 by all of the integers smaller than or equal to it, until you have exhausted all possible values.

    50 ÷ 1 = 50

    50 ÷ 2 = 25

    50 ÷ 5 = 10

    So, 50 has six positive factors: 1, 2, 5, 10, 25, and 50.

Exercise 2 (pg. 159)

1. **The correct answer is D.** Find the greatest common factor of the three numbers. Divide all the numbers by the common factor, and then multiply the dividend by the common factor to find the least common multiple.

    The greatest common factor of 80, 90, and 110 is 10.

    80 ÷ 10 = 8

    90 ÷ 10 = 9

    110 ÷ 10 = 11

    8 · 9 · 11 · 10 = 7,920

2. **The correct answer is J.** Find the greatest common factor of the three numbers. Divide all the numbers by the

common factor, and then multiply the dividend by the common factor to find the least common multiple.

The greatest common factor of 30, 130, and 80 is 10.

30 ÷ 10 = 3

130 ÷ 10 = 13

80 ÷ 10 = 8

3 · 13 · 8 · 10 = 3,120

3. **The correct answer is A.** Rewrite the numbers as the products of prime numbers. The greatest common factor will be the prime numbers that all three numbers share.

$64 = 2^6$

$80 = 2^4 \cdot 5$

$44 = 2^2 \cdot 11$

The three numbers share $2^2 = 4$ as the greatest common factor.

Exercise 3 (pg. 160)

1. The student found the greatest common divisor of 52 and 28. However, 38 is not divisible by 4. The only factor the three numbers share in common is 2. Therefore, 2 is the greatest common divisor of 52, 28, and 38.

2. It is incorrect. Factors are the numbers that 14 can be divided by resulting in a whole number quotient (the quotient is also a factor). The student missed the factor 2:

   14 ÷ 2 = 7

Exercise 4 (pg. 161)

1. Find the prime factors of each number. Then, multiply each factor by the greatest number of times it occurs in each number.

   $20 = 2^2 \cdot 5$

   17 and 5 are prime numbers.

   So, the least common multiple of 20, 17, and 5 is $2^2 \cdot 5 \cdot 17 = 340$.

2. Divide 36 by all the numbers that are smaller than 36. If the quotient is a whole number, then the divisor and the quotient are factors of 36. The factors are 1, 2, 3, 4, 6, 9, 12, 18, and 36.

Exercise 5 (pg. 162)

1. Answers will vary.

Factors, Part 2

Exercise 1 (pg. 163)

1. **The correct answer is D.** Since q is divisible by 4, look for the smallest multiple of 4 that is greater than 15 and the biggest multiple of 4 that is smaller than 75.

   $16 = 4 \cdot 4$

   $72 = 4 \cdot 18$

   There are 18 numbers below 75 that are divisible by 4. Likewise, there are 4 − 1 = 3 numbers below 15 that are divisible by 4. So, the number of possibilities that q can be are 18 − 3 = 15 possibilities.

2. **The correct answer is J.** Find the greatest common factor of the three numbers. Divide all the numbers by the common factor, and then multiply the dividend by the common factor to find the least common multiple.

   The greatest common factor of 80, 70, and 60 is 10.

   $80 \div 10 = 8 = 2^3$

   $70 \div 10 = 7$

   $60 \div 10 = 6 = 2 \cdot 3$

   $2^3 \cdot 7 \cdot 3 \cdot 10 = 1,680$

3. **The correct answer is D.** Rewrite the numbers as the product of prime numbers. Multiply the prime numbers with the largest exponents.

   $5 = 5$

   $6 = 2 \cdot 3$

   $7 = 7$

   $8 = 2^3$

   $9 = 3^2$

   $10 = 2 \cdot 5$

   The multiplication of the prime numbers with the largest exponents gives $5 \cdot 7 \cdot 2^3 \cdot 3^2 = 2,520$.

Exercise 2 (pg. 164)

1. **The correct answer is C.** Rewrite the number as the multiplication of prime numbers and their exponents.

    777 = 3 · 7 · 37

    Thus 777 is divisible by 1, 7, 37, and 3 · 7 = 21.

    11 is not one of the factors of 777.

2. **The correct answer is J.** In order to find the time when the two trains depart together, it is necessary to determine the point at which the two schedules align. Since Route A departs every 6 minutes and Route B departs every 9 minutes, determine the next time that 6 and 9 line up, specifically the least common multiple of 6 and 9.

    Rewrite the numbers as the product of prime numbers. Multiply the prime numbers with the highest exponents.

    6 = 2 · 3

    9 = 3^2

    2 · 3^2 = 18 minutes

3. **The correct answer is D.** Rewrite the numbers as the product of prime numbers. Multiply all the prime numbers using the highest exponent found from the numbers.

    24 = 2^3 · 3

    32 = 2^5

    36 = 2^2 · 3^2

    2^5 · 3^2 = 288

Exercise 3 (pg. 165)

1. Some of the numbers share a common factor, and the student did not take that into account.

    Instead of multiplying the numbers themselves, the student should multiply the prime factors of the numbers using the highest exponents that appears in the numbers.

    35 = 5 · 7

    12 = 2^2 · 3

    6 = 2 · 3

    So, the correct answer is 5 · 7 · 2^2 · 3 = 420.

2. It is incorrect. Factors are the numbers that 15 can be divided by, resulting in a whole number quotient (the quotient is also a factor). The student has 9 in the list but 15 ÷ 9 = $\frac{5}{3}$, which is not a whole number. The correct

answer is 1, 3, 5, and 15.

Exercise 4 (pg. 166)

1. Rewrite the numbers as products of prime factors. Multiply the factors that appear for all numbers.

    $40 = 2^3 \cdot 5$

    $15 = 3 \cdot 5$

    $21 = 3 \cdot 7$

    There is no common factor among the numbers, so the greatest common divisor is 1.

2. Rewrite the numbers as products of prime factors. Multiply the factors that appear for all numbers.

    $63 = 3^2 \cdot 7$

    $72 = 2^3 \cdot 3^2$

    $46 = 2 \cdot 23$

    There is no common factor among the numbers, so the greatest common divisor is 1.

Exercise 5 (pg. 167)

1. 1, 2, 3, 4, 5, 6, 10, 12, 15, 20, 25, 30, 50, 60, 75, 100, 150, 300

Fractions, Part 1

Exercise 1 (pg. 168)

1. **The correct answer is E.** Find the common denominator of all the fractions. Then, find the largest numerator. Since 3, 9, 27, 81, and 243 are all factors of 243, the common denominator is 243.

    $-\dfrac{2}{3} = -\dfrac{164}{243}$

    $-\dfrac{4}{9} = -\dfrac{108}{243}$

    $-\dfrac{8}{27} = -\dfrac{72}{243}$

    $-\dfrac{10}{81} = -\dfrac{30}{243}$

    $-\dfrac{2}{243}$

    The fraction with the largest value (least negative) is $-\dfrac{2}{243}$.

2. **The correct answer is G.** Find the decimal form of each number and compare the value.

    $\dfrac{1}{4} = 0.25$

    $0.33 = 0.33$

    $\dfrac{3}{7} \approx 0.43$

    $0.21 = 0.21$

    $\dfrac{6}{11} = 0.54$

    $\dfrac{1}{5} = 0.20$

    The ascending order is $\dfrac{1}{5}$, 0.21, $\dfrac{1}{4}$, 0.33, $\dfrac{3}{7}$, and $\dfrac{6}{11}$.

3. **The correct answer is B.** Find the common denominator of all the fractions. Then compare the numerator.

   Since 5, 9, and 11 are all factors of 495, the common denominator is 495.

   $$\frac{7}{9} = \frac{385}{495}$$

   $$\frac{3}{5} = \frac{297}{495}$$

   $$\frac{10}{11} = \frac{450}{495}$$

   So, $\frac{3}{5} < \frac{7}{9} < \frac{10}{11}$.

Exercise 2 (pg. 170)

1. **The correct answer is C.** Find the common denominator for the fractions. Add them together and divide by 2.

   $$\frac{2}{3} = \frac{6}{9}$$

   $$\frac{6}{9} + \frac{2}{9} = \frac{8}{9}$$

   $$\frac{8}{9} \div 2 = \frac{4}{9}$$

2. **The correct answer is K.** Add the whole numbers and the fractions separately. To add the fractions, find the common denominator then add the numerators.

   $5 + 3 = 8$

   $$\frac{1}{2} + \frac{3}{7} = \frac{7}{14} + \frac{6}{14} = \frac{13}{14}$$

   The snail moved $8\frac{13}{14}$ inches.

3. **The correct answer is A.** First, convert the two mixed numbers to improper fractions:

   $$2\frac{3}{4} = \frac{11}{4}$$

   and

   $$1\frac{2}{3} = \frac{5}{3}$$

   Then, find a common denominator and sum the fractions:

   $$\frac{11}{4} = \frac{33}{12}$$

   and

   $$\frac{5}{3} = \frac{20}{12}$$

   $$\frac{33}{12} + \frac{20}{12} = \frac{53}{12}$$

Next, convert the starting number of bottles of glue to have the same demominator and subtract the sum of Nick and Bobby's bottles.

$7 - \frac{53}{12}$

$\frac{84}{12} - \frac{53}{12} = \frac{31}{12}$

Finally, convert the sum to a mixed number:

$\frac{31}{12} = 2\frac{7}{12}$

Exercise 3 (pg. 172)

1. The answer is incorrect because the correct order is $\frac{2}{5} < \frac{3}{7} < \frac{1}{2}$.

   The student likely ordered the fractions by the denominator without considering the overall value of the fraction by addressing the numerator.

   The student could have found the common denominator, $5 \cdot 2 \cdot 7 = 70$, and compared the numerators.

   This would give $\frac{28}{70} < \frac{30}{70} < \frac{35}{70}$ or $\frac{2}{5} < \frac{3}{7} < \frac{1}{2}$.

2. The answer is incorrect because the student added the numerators instead of multiplying them. The student should have multiplied the denominators to get the denominator of the answer and multiplied the numerators to get the numerator of the answer. The correct answer is $\frac{3}{14}$.

Exercise 4 (pg. 174)

1. Find the common denominator of the fractions. Add the fractions.

   $\frac{3}{8} + \frac{7}{15} = \frac{45}{120} + \frac{56}{120} = \frac{101}{120}$.

2. Since Preston cut the birthday cake into 8 pieces, each piece is $\frac{1}{8}$ of the whole cake. When he eats $\frac{1}{3}$ of a piece, he eats $\frac{1}{3} \cdot \frac{1}{8} = \frac{1}{24}$ of the whole cake.

Exercise 5 (pg. 175)

1. numerator, denominator, improper fraction, least common multiple

   These words describe fractions. The numerator and denominator both describe parts of a fraction, but numerator describes the top number while denominator refers to the bottom number. An improper fraction is a type of fraction where the value of the numerator is greater than the value of the denominator. The least common multiple is used to simplify calculations with fractions and usually is used to manipulate the fractions in order to have a common denominator.

Math Elements: Middle School Bell Ringers Teacher Manual

Fractions, Part 2

Exercise 1 (pg. 176)

1. **The correct answer is E.** Change the mixed number into an improper fraction and add the fractions. Multiply by 2 and simplify the fraction.

    The common denominator is 18.

    $$\frac{4}{9} + 1\frac{1}{2} = \frac{8}{18} + \frac{27}{18} = \frac{35}{18}$$

    $$2\left(\frac{35}{18}\right) = \frac{70}{18} = 3\frac{8}{9}$$

2. **The correct answer is F.** Change the mixed numbers into improper fractions. Divide the second fraction by the first fraction to find the answer.

    $$1\frac{2}{5} \div 4\frac{4}{5} = \frac{7}{5} \div \frac{24}{5} = \frac{7}{5} \cdot \frac{5}{24} = \frac{7}{24}$$

3. **The correct answer is E.** Change each number to an improper fraction. Find the common denominator and compare.

    The common denominator is 35.

    $$5\frac{3}{5} = \frac{28}{5} = \frac{196}{35}$$

    $$5\frac{2}{7} = \frac{37}{7} = \frac{185}{35}$$

    $$-(-5.4) = \frac{189}{35}$$

    So $5\frac{2}{7} < -(-5.4) < 5\frac{3}{5}$

Exercise 2 (pg. 178)

1. **The correct answer is B.** Add the mixed numbers together by adding the whole numbers and the fractions separately. Rewrite each fraction with its common denominator. Find the range that the answer falls into.

    The common denominator is 84.

    $4 + 2 = 6$

    $$\frac{5}{12} + \frac{4}{7} = \frac{35}{84} + \frac{48}{84} = \frac{83}{84}$$

    So $4\frac{5}{12} + 2\frac{4}{7} = 6\frac{83}{84}$.

    $6\frac{83}{84}$ falls into the range between $6\frac{48}{84}$ and 7, or between $6\frac{4}{7}$ and 7

2. **The correct answer is K.** Find the common denominator and compare the numerators. The common denominator is 105.

$$-\frac{3}{5} = -\frac{63}{105}$$

$$-\frac{2}{7} = -\frac{30}{105}$$

$$-\frac{1}{3} = -\frac{35}{105}$$

The most negative fraction has the least value. So, $-\frac{3}{5} < -\frac{1}{3} < -\frac{2}{7}$.

3. **The correct answer is C.** Multiply the fraction by $\frac{1}{2}$. Multiply the numerators to get the numerator of the answer and multiply the denominators to get the denominator of the answer.

So $\frac{1}{2} \cdot \frac{2}{7} = \frac{1}{7}$

Exercise 3 (pg. 180)

1. The answer is incorrect because the correct order is $\frac{1}{9} < \frac{3}{11} < \frac{2}{5}$. The student could have found the common denominator, $5 \cdot 11 \cdot 9 = 495$, and compared the numerators.

   This would give $\frac{55}{495} < \frac{135}{495} < \frac{198}{495}$, or $\frac{1}{9} < \frac{3}{11} < \frac{2}{5}$.

2. The answer is incorrect because he added the numerator and the denominator instead of multiplying them. Notice that $\frac{6}{14} = \frac{3}{7}$. The student should have multiplied the denominators to get the denominator of the answer and multiplied the numerators to get the numerator of the answer. The correct answer is $\frac{5}{9} \cdot \frac{1}{5} = \frac{5}{45} = \frac{1}{9}$.

Exercise 4 (pg. 182)

1. Find the common denominator of the fractions. Add the fractions together to find the fraction filled by passengers.

   $$\frac{5}{7} + \frac{1}{9} = \frac{45}{63} + \frac{7}{63} = \frac{52}{63}.$$

   Subtract this answer from 1 to find the remaining unfilled space.

   $$1 - \frac{52}{63} = \frac{63}{63} - \frac{52}{63} = \frac{11}{63}$$

   So, the fraction of the train that is unfilled is $\frac{11}{63}$.

2. Since the pizza is in 6 pieces, each piece is $\frac{1}{6}$ of the whole pizza. When Thomas ate $\frac{1}{2}$ of a piece, he ate

$\frac{1}{6} \cdot \frac{1}{2} = \frac{1}{12}$ of the whole pizza. So, when Thomas ate 2 full pieces and $\frac{1}{2}$ of a piece, he ate:

$\frac{1}{6} + \frac{1}{6} + \frac{1}{12} = \frac{2}{12} + \frac{2}{12} + \frac{1}{12} = \frac{5}{12}$ of the whole pizza.

Exercise 5 (pg. 184)

1. The answer will always will be 1.

For example, consider $\frac{1}{4}$. First, divide it by $\frac{1}{3}$:

$\frac{1}{4} \div \frac{1}{3}$

$\frac{1}{4} \cdot \frac{3}{1} = \frac{3}{4}$

Next, multiply it by the reciprocal of the original fraction:

$\frac{3}{4} \cdot \frac{4}{1} = \frac{12}{4} = 3$

Then divide the result by 12.

$3 \div 12 = \frac{1}{4}$

Finally, multiply the result by 4:

$\frac{1}{4} \cdot 4 = 1$

Perimeter and Line Segments, Part 1

Exercise 1 (pg. 185)

1. **The correct answer is D.** To find the perimeter of a rectangle, add the lengths of all four of its sides. Note that rectangles have 2 sets of symmetrical lengths.

   11 + 11 + 19 + 19 = 60 inches

2. **The correct answer is F.** Set up an equation representing the perimeter in terms of the width and length. Let x represent the value of the width. Solve for x to find the width in centimeters.

   2(8) + 2(x) = 22

   16 + 2x = 22

   2x = 6

   x = 3 centimeters

3. **The correct answer is B.** The length of $\overline{BC}$ is found by subtracting the length of $\overline{AB}$ from $\overline{AC}$.

   43 − 16 = 27 inches

Exercise 2 (pg. 186)

1. **The correct answer is C.** Point Y is the midpoint of $\overline{XZ}$, and thus splits $\overline{XZ}$ into two parts of equivalent length: $\overline{XY}$ and $\overline{YZ}$. Furthermore, $\overline{XY}$ is then half of $\overline{XZ}$.

   28 ÷ 2 = 14 inches

2. **The correct answer is F.** First find the perimeter of the rectangle.

   18 + 18 + 8 + 8 = 52

   Next divide 52 by 4 to find the length of a side of a square with a perimeter of 52.

   52 ÷ 4 = 13

3. **The correct answer is D.** First find the length of the two unlabeled sides. The vertical unlabeled side is the difference of the side on the right, 11, and the side furthest to the left, 6.

   11 − 6 = 5

   The horizontal unlabeled side is the sum of the other two horizontal sides, 7 + 3 = 10.

   The perimeter is given by adding all of the labeled and unlabeled sides, 11 + 6 + 5 + 7 + 3 + 10 = 42 feet.

Exercise 3 (pg. 187)

1. 6 + 6 + 6 + 6 = 24 inches or 6 · 4 = 24 inches

2. Use the formula for the perimeter of a rectangle to solve this problem.

   $2l + 2w = P$

   $2(x + 6) + 2(x - 2) = P$

   $2x + 12 + 2x - 4 = P$

   $4x + 8 = P$

Exercise 4 (pg. 188)

1. First subtract $\overline{BC}$ from $\overline{AD}$.

   52 − 10 = 42

   Set up an equation relating the remaining length and the segment $\overline{AB}$ and $\overline{CD}$, with x representing the length of $\overline{AB}$ in inches.

   $x + 2x = 42$

   Solve for x.

   $3x = 42$

   $x = 14$

2. First find the value of the width of the rectangle. Use the formula for the perimeter of a rectangle to find the width.

   $2l + 2w = P$

   $2(14) + 2(w) = 44$

   $28 + 2w = 44$

   $2w = 16$

   $w = 8$

   The ratio of the width to the perimeter is 8:44, which can be reduced to 2:11.

Exercise 5 (pg. 189)

1. Find the perimeter of the rectangle. 0.7 + 0.7 + 0.25 + 0.25 = 1.9 miles. Then multiply this by 3 to find the total distance you will run.

   3 · 1.9 = 5.7 miles

Perimeter and Line Segments, Part 2

Exercise 1 (pg. 190)

1. **The correct answer is A.** If *B* is the midpoint of $\overline{AD}$, and $\overline{AB}$ is 5 cm, then $\overline{BD}$ is also 5 cm. Therefore, if $\overline{CD}$ is 3 cm, $\overline{BC}$ must be 2 cm.

2. **The correct answer is H.** Perimeter is the sum of all sides, so the perimeter of a rectangle is twice the length plus twice the width.

   2(12) + 2(8) = 24 + 16 = 40 inches

3. **The correct answer is B.** The total width is 12, and therefore the sum of the horizontal line segments on the top side of the figure must also total 12. The total length (7 + 3) is 10, so the total vertical line segments on the right side of the figure must also total 10. There is no way to determine the width and/or length of each of the individual line segments, but it doesn't matter because you know the total side lengths. The perimeter is the sum of all the sides, and that would be

   12 + 12 + 10 + 10 = 44 centimeters.

Exercise 2 (pg. 191)

1. **The correct answer is D.** Perimeter is the sum of all sides, so the perimeter of a rectangle is twice the length plus twice the width.

   2(24) + 2(16) = 48 + 32 = 80 feet

2. **The correct answer is H.** If the length of $\overline{VZ}$ is 10 mm, then the length of all of the sides of the square are 10 mm. The length of the sides of the triangle are also 10 mm because it is an equilateral triangle (all sides are the same), and it shares a side with the square. There are 5 total sides to the figure above, and if each side is 10 mm, then the perimeter is 50 mm.

   10 · 5 = 50 mm

3. **The correct answer is C.** If the ratio of the length of $\overline{FG}$ to $\overline{GH}$ is 2:3, then $\overline{FG}$ is 2 units and $\overline{GH}$ is 3 units. Therefore, $\overline{FH}$ is 5 units and the ratio of $\overline{FG}$ to $\overline{FH}$ is 2:5.

Exercise 3 (pg. 192)

1. If *D* is the midpoint of $\overline{AC}$ and $\overline{BD}$ is perpendicular to $\overline{AC}$, then line segment $\overline{BD}$ bisects triangle △ABC into two congruent right triangles, △ABD and △BCD. That means that triangle △ABC is isosceles, with $\overline{AB}$ and $\overline{BC}$ being the two equal sides, both 6 cm in length. The third side, $\overline{AC}$, has a length of 10 cm because $\overline{AD}$ is 5 cm and *D* is the midpoint. Therefore, the perimeter of triangle △ABC is 22 cm.

   6 + 6 + 10 = 22

2. If $\overline{BC}$ is 3 inches in length and point *B* is the midpoint of $\overline{AC}$, then $\overline{AC}$ is 6 inches in length. If point *C* is the midpoint of $\overline{AD}$, then $\overline{AD}$ is 12 inches in length. Since triangle △ADE is equilateral, all the sides are the same

length of 12 inches. Therefore, the perimeter is 36 inches.

12 + 12 + 12 = 36 inches

Exercise 4 (pg. 193)

1. If the length of $\overline{AB}$ is represented by x, then $\overline{BC}$ is $3x$, since their ratio is 1:3. Since the ratio of $\overline{AB}$ to $\overline{CD}$ is 2:3, then $\overline{CD}$ can be represented by $\frac{3}{2}x$. The ratio of $\overline{BC}$ to $\overline{CD}$ is then $3:\frac{3}{2}$, or 2:1 in simplest terms.

2. If the larger squares have a perimeter of 20 inches, then each side of each square is 5 inches. Similarly, if the square formed by the overlap has a perimeter of 8 inches, then each side is 2 inches. That means the shape formed by the overlapping squares has 4 longer sides of 5 inches each, and 4 shorter sides of 3 inches each (5-inch side of large square minus 2-inch side of smaller square). Therefore, the perimeter of the shape formed by the overlapping squares is 32 inches.

   4(5) + 4(3) = 20 + 12 = 32 inches

Exercise 5 (pg. 194)

1. Answers will vary.

Math Elements: Middle School Bell Ringers Teacher Manual

Circle Area and Circumference, Part 1

Exercise 1 (pg. 195)

1. **The correct answer is A.** Divide the diameter by 2 to find the radius. $9 \div 2 = 4\frac{1}{2}$ inches

2. **The correct answer is J.** Use the formula for the circumference of a circle to solve this problem.

   $C = 2\pi r$

   $C = 2\pi(7) = 14\pi$ inches

3. **The correct answer is B.** Use the formula for the circumference of a circle to solve this problem. Divide the diameter by 2 to find the radius. $6 \div 2 = 3$ inches.

   $C = 2\pi r$

   $C = 2\pi(3) = 6\pi \approx 18.849 \approx 19$ feet

Exercise 2 (pg. 196)

1. **The correct answer is B.** Use the formula for the area of a circle to solve this problem. Divide the diameter by 2 to find the radius. $8 \div 2 = 4$ meters

   $A = \pi r^2$

   $A = \pi(4)^2 = 16\pi$ square meters

2. **The correct answer is J.** Use the formula for the area of a circle to solve this problem. Divide the diameter by 2 to find the radius. $10 \div 2 = 5$ inches

   $A = \pi r^2$

   $A = \pi(5)^2 = 25\pi$ square inches

3. **The correct answer is C.** Use the formula for the area of a circle to solve this problem. Divide the diameter by 2 to find the radius. $12 \div 2 = 6$ centimeters

   $A = \pi r^2$

   $A = \pi(6)^2 = 36\pi$ square centimeters

Exercise 3 (pg. 197)

1. To find the circumference, use either of two formulas: $C = 2\pi r$, or $C = d\pi$, where r = radius and d = diameter. The diameter of the circle is already given, and the radius is equal to half the diameter: $r = \frac{20}{2} = 10$.

   $C = 2\pi r = 2\pi(10) = 20\pi$

$C = d\pi = (20)\pi = 20\pi$

The circumference of the circle is 20π inches.

2. The student likely used the formula for the circumference of a circle ($C = 2\pi r$), instead of using the formula for the area of a circle ($A = \pi r^2$).

    Plug in the value for the radius into the formula for the area of a circle to find the correct answer:

    $A = \pi r^2$

    $A = \pi(5)^2 = 25\pi$

    The area of the circle is 25π square inches.

Exercise 4 (pg. 198)

1. Plug in the value of the radius into the formula for the area of a circle to find the correct answer:

    $A = \pi r^2$

    $A = \pi(8)^2 = 64\pi$

    The area of the circle is 64π square inches.

2. The student likely plugged the value of the diameter, instead of the radius, into the formula for the circumference of a circle.

    To find the circumference, use either of two formulas: $C = 2\pi r$, or $C = d\pi$, where r = radius and d = diameter. The diameter of the circle is already given, and the radius is equal to half the diameter: $r = \dfrac{12}{2} = 6$ inches.

    $C = 2\pi r = 2\pi(6) = 12\pi$

    $C = d\pi = (12)\pi = 12\pi$

    The circumference of the circle is 12π inches.

Exercise 5 (pg. 199)

1. Find the area of each pizza using the formula $A = \pi r^2$.

    Charley's Pizza: $A = \pi 5^2 \approx 79$ in^2

    Nicole's Pizza: $A = \pi 6^2 \approx 113$ in^2

    The price of a large pizza at Charley's Pizza is $12 per 79 in^2, or
    $12 \div 79 \approx 15$ cents per square inch. The price of a large pizza at Nicole's Pizza is $15 per 113 in^2, or $15 \div 113 \approx 13$ cents per square inch. Nicole's Pizza has the better deal.

Math Elements: Middle School Bell Ringers Teacher Manual

Circle Area and Circumference, Part 2

Exercise 1 (pg. 200)

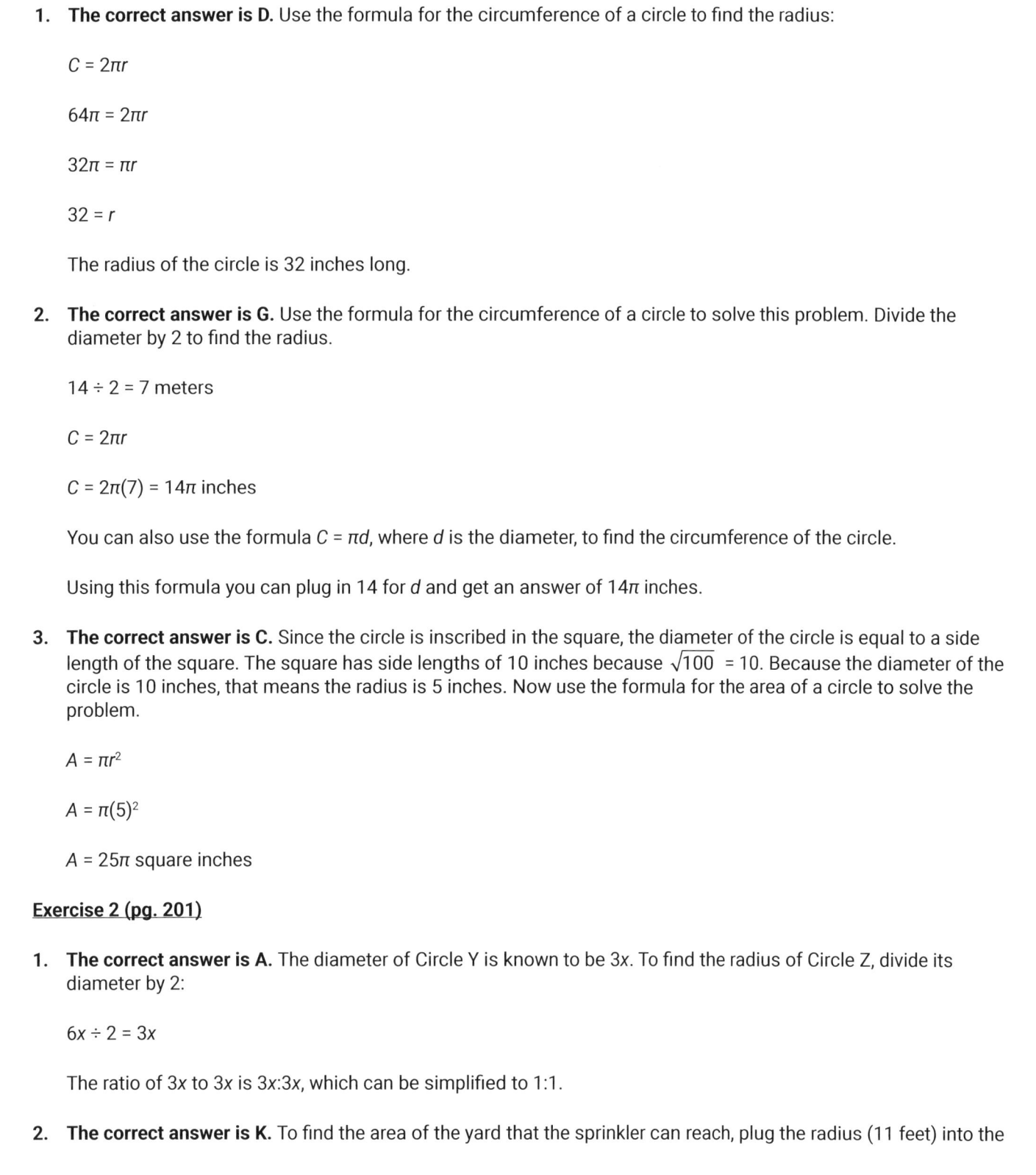

1. **The correct answer is D.** Use the formula for the circumference of a circle to find the radius:

   $C = 2\pi r$

   $64\pi = 2\pi r$

   $32\pi = \pi r$

   $32 = r$

   The radius of the circle is 32 inches long.

2. **The correct answer is G.** Use the formula for the circumference of a circle to solve this problem. Divide the diameter by 2 to find the radius.

   $14 \div 2 = 7$ meters

   $C = 2\pi r$

   $C = 2\pi(7) = 14\pi$ inches

   You can also use the formula $C = \pi d$, where d is the diameter, to find the circumference of the circle.

   Using this formula you can plug in 14 for d and get an answer of 14π inches.

3. **The correct answer is C.** Since the circle is inscribed in the square, the diameter of the circle is equal to a side length of the square. The square has side lengths of 10 inches because $\sqrt{100} = 10$. Because the diameter of the circle is 10 inches, that means the radius is 5 inches. Now use the formula for the area of a circle to solve the problem.

   $A = \pi r^2$

   $A = \pi(5)^2$

   $A = 25\pi$ square inches

Exercise 2 (pg. 201)

1. **The correct answer is A.** The diameter of Circle Y is known to be $3x$. To find the radius of Circle Z, divide its diameter by 2:

   $6x \div 2 = 3x$

   The ratio of $3x$ to $3x$ is $3x:3x$, which can be simplified to 1:1.

2. **The correct answer is K.** To find the area of the yard that the sprinkler can reach, plug the radius (11 feet) into the

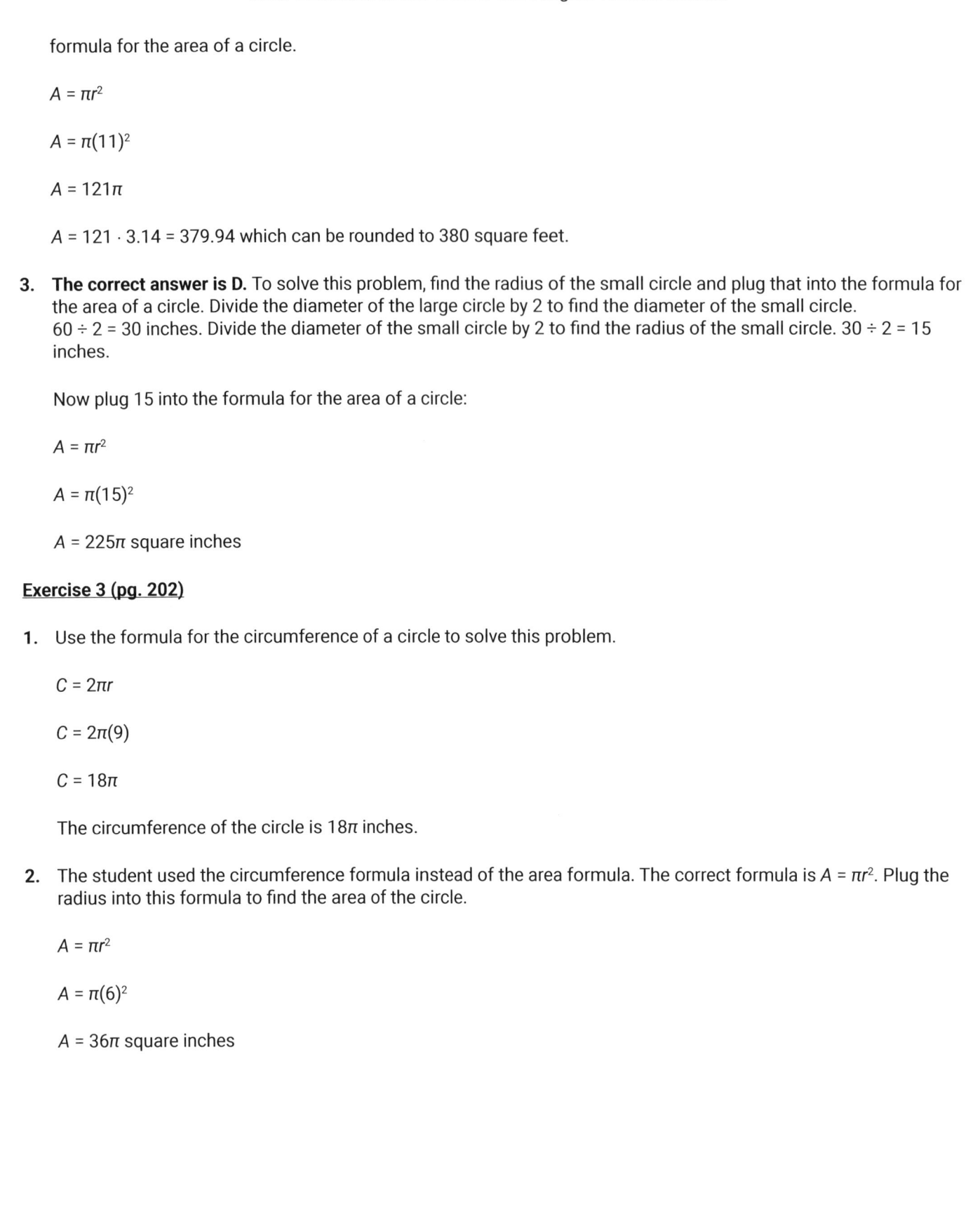

formula for the area of a circle.

$A = \pi r^2$

$A = \pi(11)^2$

$A = 121\pi$

$A = 121 \cdot 3.14 = 379.94$ which can be rounded to 380 square feet.

3. **The correct answer is D.** To solve this problem, find the radius of the small circle and plug that into the formula for the area of a circle. Divide the diameter of the large circle by 2 to find the diameter of the small circle. $60 \div 2 = 30$ inches. Divide the diameter of the small circle by 2 to find the radius of the small circle. $30 \div 2 = 15$ inches.

   Now plug 15 into the formula for the area of a circle:

   $A = \pi r^2$

   $A = \pi(15)^2$

   $A = 225\pi$ square inches

Exercise 3 (pg. 202)

1. Use the formula for the circumference of a circle to solve this problem.

   $C = 2\pi r$

   $C = 2\pi(9)$

   $C = 18\pi$

   The circumference of the circle is 18π inches.

2. The student used the circumference formula instead of the area formula. The correct formula is $A = \pi r^2$. Plug the radius into this formula to find the area of the circle.

   $A = \pi r^2$

   $A = \pi(6)^2$

   $A = 36\pi$ square inches

Exercise 4 (pg. 203)

1. First, find the radius of the circle by using the formula for the area of a circle.

   $A = \pi r^2$

   $625\pi = \pi r^2$

   $625 = r^2$

   $25 = r$

   Now multiply the radius by 2 to find the diameter: $25 \cdot 2 = 50$.

   The diameter of the circle is 50 inches.

2. First, find the radius of the circle by using the formula for the area of a circle.

   $A = \pi r^2$

   $361\pi = \pi r^2$

   $361 = r^2$

   $19 = r$

   Now use the formula for the circumference of a circle to solve this problem.

   $C = 2\pi r$

   $C = 2\pi(19) = 38\pi$

   The circumference of the circle is 38π inches.

Exercise 5 (pg. 204)

1. Pumpkin pi

   Explanations will vary.

Math Elements: Middle School Bell Ringers Teacher Manual

Deconstructing Geometric Figures

Exercise 1 (pg. 205)

1. **The correct answer is C.** Start by breaking the figure into 2 rectangles. The first rectangle is created by the top section and has dimensions of 10 by 30. The second rectangle is created by the remaining area of the figure, and has dimensions of 10 by 20. The total area is found by finding the area of both rectangles and adding them.

    $10 \cdot 30 = 300$

    $10 \cdot 20 = 200$

    $300 + 200 = 500$ square feet

2. **The correct answer is G.** Compute the area by finding the area of both the triangle on the left and the square on the right and adding them.

    Area of the triangle: $A = \frac{1}{2}(b)(h)$

    $A = \frac{1}{2}(6)(8) = 24$

    Area of the square: $A = s^2$

    $A = 8^2 = 64$

    Area of the figure: $24 + 64 = 88$ square centimeters

3. **The correct answer is C.** Split the figure into 3 rectangles dividing the sections by the three widths created by the bottom of the figure. The first rectangle is on the left side of the figure and is given by the dimensions 12 by 5. The second rectangle is created by the right side and the bottom measurement, and is, thus, 10 by 5. The third rectangle is created by the middle section of the bottom of the figure and the sides of the other rectangles, and is, thus, 2 by 7. The whole area is found by adding all three areas.

    $12 \cdot 5 = 60$

    $5 \cdot 10 = 50$

    $2 \cdot 7 = 14$

    $60 + 50 + 14 = 124$ square feet

Exercise 2 (pg. 207)

1. **The correct answer is D.** Start by breaking the figure into a smaller square and a larger rectangle, the square comprised of the small area protruding from the top right of the figure. Solve for the area of the small square by multiplying the given side lengths. $1\frac{3}{4} \cdot 1\frac{3}{4} = 3\frac{1}{16}$

   Solve for the area of the large rectangle by multiplying 3 by the sum of the two measurements on the right sides. $(3) \cdot (1\frac{3}{4} + 1\frac{3}{4}) = 10\frac{1}{2}$. Find the area of the whole figure by adding the two areas.

   $3\frac{1}{16} + 10\frac{1}{2} = 13\frac{9}{16}$

2. **The correct answer is J.** Start by finding the area of the square.

   $A = 4 \cdot 4 = 16$

   Next find the area of the circle and subtract this from the area of the square.

   $A = \pi(2)^2 = 4\pi$

   $A = 16 - 4\pi$

   Finally, divide this value by 2, as the shaded region is only half of the difference between the square and circle.

   Area of the shaded region: $(16 - 4\pi) \div 2 = 8 - 2\pi$

3. **The correct answer is A.** Start by splitting the figure into two rectangles, one 10 by 5 on the right and one 5 by 6 on the left.

   $5 \cdot 6 = 30$

   $10 \cdot 5 = 50$

   Add the values to find the total area.

   $30 + 50 = 80$ square feet

   Find the amount of sod by dividing the total area by the area covered by an individual bag.

   $80 \div 50 = 1.6$ packs of sod

   Since a fraction of a pack cannot be purchased, John must purchase 2 packs.

Exercise 3 (pg. 209)

1. Start the problem by finding the lengths of the unlabeled sides of the house. The unlabeled length on the right side is 15 feet, as the total side length is 25, and the other right wall is 10 feet long. The bottom length is found by subtracting the 25 foot wall from the 45 foot wall total, leaving 20 feet.

25 + 45 + 15 + 25 + 10 + 20 = 140 feet

Next multiply the perimeter by the height of the house to find the total surface area being painted.

140 · 10 = 1,400 square feet

Finally divide the total surface area by the amount of area that a can of paint covers to find the number of cans of paint needed.

1,400 ÷ 500 = 2.8

Therefore, Bill must purchase 3 cans of paint.

2. The area of the figure is found by computing the areas of the two triangles individually and then adding them together. Use the formula for the area of a triangle: $A = \frac{1}{2}(b)(h)$

$\frac{1}{2} \cdot 4 \cdot 2 = 4$ square feet

$\frac{1}{2} \cdot 4 \cdot 8 = 16$ square feet

16 + 4 = 20 square feet

Exercise 4 (pg. 211)

1. First find the area of the circle.

$A = \pi(4)^2 = 16\pi$

Then, subtract the area of the triangle from the area of the circle and divide by three to find the area of the shaded region.

$A = \frac{16\pi - 12\sqrt{3}}{3}$ square feet

2. To find the perimeter of the property the unlabeled sides must be labeled. The bottom unlabeled side is 10 meters, as it is shown in the parts above labeled 6 and 4. The top diagonal unlabeled side is found by first finding its small height on the left. The small height is found by subtracting the 4 and 10 sections from the total left height of 15, leaving 1. The diagonal length is then found using Pythagorean Theorem.

$1^2 + 4^2 = c^2$

$c = \sqrt{1^2 + 4^2} = \sqrt{17}$

Finally, add together all of the pieces of the polygon.

$10 + 10 + 6 + 4 + \sqrt{17} + 15 = 45 + \sqrt{17}$ meters

Exercise 5 (pg. 213)

1. Answers will vary. Students should recognize that they can divide the shape into smaller, simpler shapes for which they know how to find area. This shape could be divided into rectangles and triangles. The area of all of the smaller shapes could then be calculated and added together to find the area of the entire shape.

Math Elements: Middle School Bell Ringers Teacher Manual

Measurement Relationships

Exercise 1 (pg. 214)

1. **The correct answer is C.** Start by creating an equation to represent the perimeter of the square is terms of the side lengths, using the variable *x* to represent the length of the side.

    36 = 4*x*

    Solve the equation, and use the side length to find the area of the square.

    9 = *x*

    A = 9 · 9 = 81

    Therefore, the area of the square is 81 square centimeters.

2. **The correct answer is J.** Start by creating a system of equations representing the area and perimeter of the rectangle with variables *x* and *y* to represent the length and width.

    2(*x* + *y*) = 32

    xy = 48

    Solve the system for the two variables and the answer is the larger of the two values.

    x + *y* = 16

    x = 16 − *y*

    (16 − *y*)(*y*) = 48

    *y*² − 16*y* + 48 = 0

    y = 12, *y* = 4

    If *y* = 12, then *x* = 4. If *y* = 4, then *x* = 12. Thus the larger of the two side lengths of the rectangle is 12 yards.

    If you are unsure about how to solve this problem, try plugging in the answer choices.

3. **The correct answer is D.** Start by creating an equation to represent the perimeter of the square fence using the variable *x* to represent the side length of the square.

    4*x* = 20

    Solve for the side length.

    x = 5

    Given the side length of the square fence, find the area of the fence.

A = 5 · 5 = 25

Therefore, the area enclosed by the fence is 25 square feet.

Exercise 2 (pg. 215)

1. **The correct answer is C.** Start by creating an equation to represent the volume of the box in terms of length, height, and width. Use the variable w to represent the value of the width and the values given in the question to represent the other variables.

   $V = l \cdot h \cdot w$

   $9{,}000 = 20 \cdot 15 \cdot w$

   Solve the equation for the value of w.

   $9{,}000 = 300 \cdot w$

   $w = 30$

   Therefore, the width of the box is 30 centimeters.

2. **The correct answer is J.** Start by creating an equation to represent the perimeter of the space in terms of the variable l, representing the value of the length.

   $100 = (2)(l) + (2)(l - 20)$

   Solve for l.

   $4l - 40 = 100$

   $4l = 140$

   $l = 35$

   The length is thus 35 inches. Solve for the width using the representation of the width in terms of length and replacing the variable with the newly found value.

   $35 - 20 = 15$

   Therefore, the width is 15 inches, and the dimensions of the rectangular space are 15 by 35.

3. **The correct answer is C.** Start by creating an equation representing the area of Bob's house with the information given and the variable l to represent the length of the house.

   $500 = 25 \cdot l$

   Solve for l.

   $l = 20$

Add together the sides of the house not touching Alex's house, that is 2 lengths and one width.

A = 20 + 20 + 25 = 65

Therefore, the combined length is 65 meters.

Exercise 3 (pg. 216)

1. Start by creating a system of equations with length and width represented with *x* and *y*, respectively.

    24 = x · y

    20 = 2(x + y)

    Solve for one of the variables and use substitution to obtain the value of the other.

    10 = x + y

    y = 10 − x

    24 = (x)(10 − x)

    x^2 − 10x + 24 = 0

    x = 6 and x = 4

    y = 4 and y = 6

    Thus, the dimensions, in feet, of the rectangle are 4 and 6.

2. In order to solve for the missing length value, set up an equation representing the volume of the box in terms of length, width, and height, with the variable *l* representing the length. Solve for the variable to find the length in inches.

    24,000 = 30 · 40 · *l*

    24,000 ÷ 1,200 = *l*

    l = 20

    Therefore the length of the box is 20 inches.

Exercise 4 (pg. 217)

1. Start by solving for the side length of a square with an area of 400 square feet by setting up the following equation with *s* representing the side length.

    $s^2 = 400$

    $20 = s$

    Solve for the perimeter of the square with side length 20 using the following equation.

    $4 \cdot s = ?$

    $4 \cdot 20 = 80$

    Therefore, the perimeter of the square fence is 80 feet.

2. Start by setting up an equation representing the perimeter of the rectangle in terms of the variable *y*, which represents the width of the rectangle. Solve the equation for the width.

    $80 = 2y + 2(\frac{1}{4}y)$

    $2.5y = 80$

    $y = 32$

    Given the width of the rectangle, solve for the length with the given relation between the length and width.

    $32 \div 4 = 8$

    Given a length of 8 feet and a width of 32 feet, solve for the area of the rectangle by multiplying the values.

    $32 \cdot 8 = 256$ square feet

Exercise 5 (pg. 218)

1. Answers will vary.

Volume, Part 1

Exercise 1 (pg. 219)

1. **The correct answer is E.** Use the formula for the volume of a rectangular prism:

    $V = l \cdot w \cdot h$

    $V = 12 \cdot 8 \cdot 5$

    $V = 480$ cubic inches

2. **The correct answer is J.** Use the formula for the volume of a cube:

    $V = s^3$

    $V = (5)^3 = 125$ cubic centimeters

3. **The correct answer is C.** Use the formula for the volume of a rectangular prism:

    $V = l \cdot w \cdot h$

    $2{,}205 = 15 \cdot 21 \cdot h$

    $2{,}205 = 315h$

    $h = 7$ feet

Exercise 2 (pg. 220)

1. **The correct answer is B.** Use the formula for the volume of a rectangular prism:

    $V = l \cdot w \cdot h$

    $106{,}920 = 66 \cdot 54 \cdot h$

    $106{,}920 = 3{,}564h$

    $h = 30$ inches

2. **The correct answer is H.** Use the formula for the volume of a cylinder:

    $V = \pi r^2 h$

    $V = \pi(8)^2(10) = 640\pi$ cubic feet

3. **The correct answer is C.** Use the formula for the volume of a cube to find the volume of one of the cubes and then multiply by 3 to find the total volume.

$V = s^3$

$V = (3)^3 = 27$ cubic centimeters

$27 \cdot 3 = 81$ cubic centimeters

Exercise 3 (pg. 221)

1. If the volume of the smaller cube is 12 and the larger cube has a height three times that of the smaller cube, then taking the volume of the smaller cube to the third power would produce a larger, incorrect volume. Instead, the volume of the smaller cube can be multiplied by 3^3, resulting in a volume of $12 \cdot 27 = 324$ in^3.

2. The area of a rectangular prism is the area of its base (the width multiplied by the length) times its height. The base of the rectangular prism is 16 square inches, so dividing by 16 twice is incorrect. The student should have divided the volume, 128, by the base, 16, only once to get a height of 8 inches.

Exercise 4 (pg. 222)

1. All edges of a cube are the same length. If one edge is x, every edge must also be x. A cube is a three dimensional solid which means it has a length, width, and height. The expression accounts for all three dimensions being multiplied together to calculate the volume. Therefore, the volume must be x^3.

2. Height x for the cylinder represents the capacity of the container. To measure the true volume of the liquid, measure the height of the liquid within the cylinder, which would be expressed by the formula $\pi r^2 y$.

Exercise 5 (pg. 223)

1. First find the volume of the water basin. $9 \cdot 20 \cdot 5 = 900$ ft^3

   Subtract the amount of water that is already in the basin. $900 - 700 = 200$. You need 200 more cubic feet of water for the basin.

   Calculate the volume of your carton. $1 \cdot 2 \cdot 3 = 6$ ft^3

   Divide the amount of water you need by how big your carton is. $200 \div 6 \approx 33.333$ so you will need to make 34 trips to completely fill up the water basin.

Volume, Part 2

Exercise 1 (pg. 224)

1. **The correct answer is C.** Use the formula to find the volume of the cylinder.

   $V = \pi r^2 h$

   $V = \pi(9)^2(15)$

   $V = \pi(81)(15)$

   $V = 1,215\pi \approx 3,817$ cubic centimeters

2. **The correct answer is H.** Use the formula to find the volume of the rectangular prism.

   $V = lwh$

   Since the height and the width are the same we can assign them x. Therefore, the length is equal to $3x$. Plug these values into the formula.

   $375 = x \cdot x \cdot 3x$

   $375 = 3x^3$

   $125 = x^3$

   $5 = x$

   We know that the height and width are both 5 centimeters, so the length must be $5 \cdot 3 = 15$ centimeters long.

3. **The correct answer is E.** Since Cube X has sides that are 3 centimeters long and Cube Y has sides that are three times longer than Cube X, then Cube Y must have sides that are 9 centimeters long. Therefore, the volume of Cube Y is $(9)^3 = 729$ cubic centimeters.

Exercise 2 (pg. 226)

1. **The correct answer is B.** Find the area of the triangular face and multiply that by the length of the prism.

   $A = \dfrac{1}{2}bh$

   $A = \dfrac{1}{2}(5)(4)$

   $A = (5)(2) = 10$

   $V = 10 \cdot 8 = 80$ cubic inches

2. **The correct answer is F.** Use the formula for the volume of a sphere to solve this problem. Since the diameter is

12, the radius is 6 inches.

$V = \dfrac{4}{3} \pi r^3$

$V = \dfrac{4}{3} \pi (6)^3$

$V = \dfrac{4}{3} \pi (216) = 288\pi$ cubic inches

3. **The correct answer is D.** Use the formula to find the volume of the cylinder. Since the glass is only filled to a depth of 6 centimeters, use 6 as the height instead of 10.

$V = \pi r^2 h$

$V = \pi (8)^2 (6)$

$V = \pi (64)(6)$

$V = 384\pi \approx 1{,}206$ cubic centimeters

Exercise 3 (pg. 228)

1. The volume of a cylinder is calculated by finding the area, not circumference, of the circle that forms the base of the cylinder and multiplying that number by the height. The student should have squared the radius, multiplied that result by π, and then multiplied that result by the height. $4^2(\pi)5$ equals 80π.

2. The student forgot the formula for the area of a triangle, the base of the prism. When calculating the area of the base of the triangle, it is important to remember to use $\dfrac{1}{2}bh$. With a base of 4 and a height of 5, this would be set up $\dfrac{1}{2}(4)(5)$. This gives 10 for the area. Multiplying that result by a length of 9 would produce a result of 90.

Exercise 4 (pg. 229)

1. Even though two triangles comprise a triangle, there is still only one base. When calculating the volume of a triangular prism, first calculate the area of the triangle that makes up the base. The formula, $\dfrac{1}{2}bh$, stays the same.

2. The first step in calculating the volume of a sphere is to plug in the missing number of the radius. Then, the radius must be cubed. No other operation can be performed until the radius cubed is calculated. Next, the cubed radius must be multiplied by 4. Finally, the result must be divided by 3. If the answer choices include π, there is no need to multiply by π. If the answer choices include whole numbers without π, the last step is to multiply by π and round to the nearest whole number.

Exercise 5 (pg. 230)

1. volume, radius, height, cylinder

   Volume refers to the total amount of space taken up by a three dimensional object. To find the volume of a cylinder, you must first find the values for the radius and the height.